3/14

More Praise for Tovah Klein and *How Toddlers Thrive*

"In this wonderful book, Tovah Klein draws on her deep understanding of toddlers and their development to offer a treasure trove of wise and practical advice. Placing a special emphasis on seeing the world through toddlers' eyes, Klein shows how we can help them meet life's challenges with confidence and enthusiasm. *How Toddlers Thrive* will be cherished by parents and professionals alike."

—William Crain, author of *Reclaiming Childhood: Letting Children Be Children in Our Achievement-Oriented Society*

"If only there was one single, sensible, sympathetic book that answered all your toddler questions. Well there is. And you're holding it: an easy-to-read source that explains what toddlers do, why they do it, and whether you have to jump in or not. The good news is: Often the answer is 'not.' "

—Lenore Skenazy, author of *Free-Range Kids: How to Raise Safe, Self-Reliant Kids (Without Going Nuts with Worry)*

"You survived your baby's infancy and you're about to give a sigh of relief (and maybe get some sleep) when toddlerhood hits you like a ton of bricks. Trust Tovah Klein to help you navigate those confusing—and sometimes infuriating—years from two to five. This is a compassionate book that helps parents see the world from a toddler's point of view, which in turn leads to more successful and relaxed parenting."

—Lawrence J. Cohen, PhD, author of *The Opposite of Worry* and *Playful Parenting*

"Dr. Klein has provided a critical resource for parents—she combines state-of-the-science research with examples of and practical guidelines for everyday toddler-parent interactions. Most important, Dr. Klein appreciates that every toddler and parent is unique, and therefore, there is no single parenting 'recipe.' Instead, *How Toddlers Thrive* offers a perspective that appreciates the variability in approaches that parents could take. This book is valuable for parents and researchers alike."

—Nim Tottenham, PhD, developmental neuroscientist at the University of California, Los Angeles

"There are a lot of parenting books out there, but this one is unique—it's told from the point of view of the child! Dr. Klein's firsthand experience with young children provides parents an understanding of child development within the context of family dynamics. She doesn't judge parents; instead she empowers them with knowledge about the whys behind their children's behaviors."

—Rosemarie T. Truglio, PhD, SVP of Curriculum and Content for Sesame Workshop

How Toddlers Thrive

What Parents Can Do Today for Children Ages 2–5 to Plant the Seeds of Lifelong Success

Tovah P. Klein, PhD

A TOUCHSTONE BOOK
Published by Simon & Schuster
New York London Toronto Sydney New Delhi

Touchstone
A Division of Simon & Schuster, Inc.
1230 Avenue of the Americas
New York, NY 10020

First Touchstone hardcover edition February 2014

Interior design by Aline Pace
Jacket design by Eileen Carey
Jacket photograph © Laura Flugga/E+/Getty Images

Manufactured in the United States of America

10 9 8 7 6 5 4 3 2 1

Library of Congress Control Number: 2013032839

ISBN 978-1-4767-3513-9
ISBN 978-1-4767-3515-3 (ebook)

For Pat, my dear friend and toddler partner

and

For my own former toddlers, Elam, Aaron, and Jesse, with love

Contents

Foreword by Sarah Jessica Parker

I come from a big family. My childhood memories include plenty of playful days, and lots of siblings taking care of one another, serving as extra sets of hands for my parents. We were very loved but also allowed to be independent. I became a mother to a much smaller brood, and initially approached mothering my first child (and then the other two) with as much intensity and fierce determination as my mother had given all of her eight kids combined. All the while I was feeling—like many mothers—that I wasn't doing enough. Then I met Tovah Klein and realized that my mother may have had it right all along. Tovah taught me that the space given to children raised in a big, bustling family may actually do a better job giving them a sense of self, of self-respect, and of confidence in their own accomplishments. Tovah taught me how to resist the temptation to fix everything, and instead give my children the opportunity to learn how to problem-solve for themselves.

My three children are all different, but my husband and I have the tools to parent each of them in ways that work for them. One is outgoing, another cried and cried whenever I left her at school, and another is cut-and-dried. Tovah taught me that there is no one right way to parent, and no right way for children to experience childhood. Judging myself or the child risks inadvertently imposing a feeling of shame that does more to set back than to help. Tovah's parenting approach enabled me to get inside the complicated mind of my then two-year-olds; to give choices, but not too many; to establish order and still give them freedom. I went from feeling overwhelmed to feeling confident, all while giving my children their own sense of confidence in themselves, which I see further developing as they grow. I hope the same for you and your children. Enjoy!

Introduction

I live in toddler-dom. As the director of the internationally renowned Barnard College Center for Toddler Development (known as the Toddler Center), I have the pleasure of living in a world of toddlers and seeing the world from their perspective. It is a different and often entertaining view of the world. I have now worked at this magical place for almost two decades and spend five days a week thinking about, observing, studying, and interacting with fifty individual toddlers.

I teach undergraduate and graduate students about them, help parents understand what is going on with them and why they do what they do. I also conduct studies on separation, play, sleep, and other important aspects of toddler development, and all the while I get to watch toddlers be toddlers. My work focuses on understanding what young children do and the role parents play in their development. Whether watching, researching, or interacting directly with children, I am asking myself the question—over and over—*what are they doing, and why are they doing it?*

• What Are They Doing? •

The first question—*what are they doing?*—is deceptively straightforward. It seems to many parents like toddlers are simply starting to practice the basic skills that they'll need for the future, whether that's learning how to brush their teeth, figuring out how to share, or understanding how to sit at a table and eat during a meal. Mastering these kinds of essential tasks is a big part of what these years are about. But as I've learned during my decades working with kids from ages two to five, there's a lot more going on in their brains than their behaviors lead us to believe.

The toddler years (which, for the purposes of this book, I'm defining as ages two to five) are among the least studied years in childhood. Compared to the numbers of studies of infants and school-aged kids, toddlers have historically gotten short shrift, which is alarming given the fact that during this time period, the brain and body are in a massive state of flux, growth, and change. Indeed, the toddler brain is enormously complex and dynamic, going through as much upheaval and adaptations as the teenage brain. Toddlers are not just learning how to use the toilet or tame a tantrum—they are actually learning some crucially important life skills that are the keys to their later success. It's during these intense toddler years that a child's brain lays down pathways needed for him or her to thrive throughout childhood and life.

I like to call the toddler years a "lab for later." That's because many of the basic skills that parents are helping to nurture and teach their children during the toddler years are actually preparing those children's young brains to take on higher-level types of learning. For example, I always tell my families about the importance of establishing a bedtime ritual: taking a bath, brushing the teeth, maybe reading a book, and then off to sleep. All these seemingly basic tasks are part of a network of skills that are crucial for toddlers to master. But there is also learning to be had in establishing the routine itself, and in varying it. What if one day, the parent decides to brush the child's teeth before the bath rather than after it? How will a toddler handle such a change? Will she have a tantrum (*That's NOT how we do it!*) or will she have the flexibility and resilience to accept a change in routine? Helping your child to develop this ability to adapt will not only make your life as a parent a little smoother, but it will also make your child ready to tackle the unforeseen changes she will most certainly face at school and in the world.

It's these types of higher-level skills—including resilience, cooperation, self-reliance, determination, perseverance, empathy, and more—that toddler brains are ready to start developing. In fact, the toddler brain is hardwired to learn these skills that are the foundation of self-regulation, and what's more, it's up to us as parents and educators to help them learn how to do so. But it takes time and practice to learn these skills. That's why the toddler years are a lab for later: the earlier kids become familiar and comfortable with these skills, the happier and more successful they will be. That's the promise of this book.

• Why Are They Doing It? •

The second question—*why are they doing it?*—often seems more complex than it really is. In other words, once you start to observe and understand your toddler, you'll be able to understand (and sometimes even anticipate) their reactions and their concerns. I call this "seeing the world through your toddler's eyes," or your Parenting POV (point of view). It's when we as adults shift our view from seeing the world through an adult perspective to that of a child's perspective—a shift that can happen immediately or take some time. When this happens, we suddenly are in a position to support our children in a way that is clear and much, much easier to carry out. Why is seeing the world from a child's point of view so important? Because that's the best way to understand them, to guide them with love and encouragement, and to avoid shaming and controlling them. When we use this Parenting POV, we are able to be aware and compassionate to the needs of our young children; we are also able to give them the limits and boundaries they require to navigate this tumultuous time. We give them the love and limits without the fights!

My "Parenting POV" approach has been successful for the many hundreds of families I have come to know through both the Toddler Center and the parenting groups I meet with on an ongoing basis—and for individual parents who are facing a particular rough spot or challenge with their child. Some of these parents return long after their kids have left the Toddler Center. Why? Because even after a child has moved beyond the toddler years, challenges with changing behavior and needs still arise. Many parents come back knowing I can continue to help them understand who their child is and figure out what their child needs as they grow.

My parenting POV approach is based on the continually evolving body of psychological and neuroscience research on this age, combined with the research and observations I have done for more than twenty years. It's designed to maximize the emotional, social, and cognitive development of toddlers. My approach sits firmly at the intersection of knowing the science and applying it to support children in a way so that all parents and their children may benefit. No one brain study or even a few can answer all of our questions about our child's development, and I caution you to be careful about jumping to conclusions from any single study or two. It takes many years of research to reveal what specific details mean more broadly about how children develop. What I've tried to do here is pull together the most consistent scientific findings and understandings about how to help your toddler thrive and succeed, today and in the future.

• Dealing with the Day-to-Day •

The parents I work with are an eclectic array of thoughtful, creative, and caring parents. There are two-parent families and single-parent families; there are families with working parents and some with one parent at home; some of the families have grandparents living with them and others have recently moved here from other countries. Some families are small, with one or two children, and some are large, with three or more children. But what they all have in common with one another, and with you, is an intense desire to parent in the best way they can so their children can be the best they can be! Parenting toddlers involves both "high-level" and "day-to-day" skills: we are trying to help our children develop resilience, manage their intense emotions, and figure out who they are in this world (the skills that set the foundation for self-regulation). At the same time, we are trying to help them with the everyday tasks such as getting up and out the door in the morning, going to bed without a fuss, and getting through mealtimes and transitions without tantrums and meltdowns. Of course, these high-level and day-to-day skills are deeply interconnected, as you will see. Every parent struggles at some point, and even at many points; there are also commonalities about what parents struggle with, even though every family is unique: sleep, eating, meltdowns, fears, sibling conflicts, not listening, being rude, talking back, regression, thumb sucking, throwing toys, nervous habits, hitting, biting, or kicking. In the end, we all grapple with what to do and how to help our child.

As is typical these days, many of the parents with whom I consult are stressed, doing their best to juggle all the aspects of their lives. They are also worried and self-doubting about decisions they have to make about their kids, wondering if they should pay attention to their gut about what's best or listen to an expert or a well-meaning friend or their own parents. A couple was struggling with how to get their child to sleep through the night. They came to see me and presented it this way, "He is four now. We've tried it all. The pediatrician said to use a sticker chart. That worked for a few nights, then stopped. We tried bribing with doughnuts for breakfast. My best friend suggested this special lullaby CD. We've locked his door. We've explained why he needs to sleep. Nothing works. I've read all kinds of things on the Web, and now I am worried he may have some serious problem causing the sleep issues." I asked what they thought, in their hearts, was the best solution. After a long pause, the father said, "We just don't know. We don't know who to trust." With unlimited information on the Web, I find parents are more self-doubting than ever. I do understand why. Parenting can feel like a competitive arena, rather than the very personal process that it is.

Is it okay that he uses a pacifier at night? How much sugar can she have each day? How much TV is too much? Is the iPad going to make my child smarter? What is the best type of preschool for a three-year-old? How do I get her to eat a bigger variety of foods? Is it normal to tantrum as much as my child does? Why does he go crazy just because we are out of the cereal he wants? Is it normal for him to grab another child's toy and just walk away? Why doesn't she join in and play at birthday parties? How can I be sure she learns how to make friends? What is normal behavior at this age?

They have questions related to their children's behavior, their difficulty sticking to a routine, getting along with other kids, or turning into what the parents were hoping for: happy, engaged, thoughtful little people ready to conquer the world.

Like you, these parents always want what's best for their children. They are dedicated and devoted, smart and considerate. And once they begin to trust in this approach, their whole way of thinking about parenting shifts. They not only grasp how to handle the day-to-day toddler moments with ease; they also understand why parenting during the toddler years is so important to their children's later development. But perhaps most important of all, they come to understand how parents have a crucial role in the best possible outcome for their children, for now and for when they grow into bigger kids, teens, and eventually adults. Toddler-dom is indeed a marvelous opportunity—a true lab for later. As one mother, Jocelyn, said, "I learned how my daughter is thinking and why she is doing what she is doing—it used to be so easy for me to get frustrated before I understood the world through her eyes."

Another parent, Martha Ann, said, "There is so much pressure to raise kids; I've learned that it's good for them to be bored, that it's best that they are not overscheduled and to give them a lot of downtime." One mom revealed, "Sometimes it is so embarrassing what kids say, but it's better to say to yourself, 'What's the best way to handle this situation?' Instead of trying to shut down my child because she said someone smelled bad." And another mom, Sally, put it, "It's so liberating! I don't over-parent anymore! I don't feel the need to constantly interfere between siblings, and I can back off and let my kids be themselves!" Following an initial session with a couple, the father returned the next week and said, "You've saved us from ourselves. As first-time parents, we kept thinking our two-year-old should share and be nice. That is how we were raised. We felt so pressured. But now I see he can't share at this age. I am relieved and enjoying him more. And he is happier."

When parents shift their view and learn to understand the world through the eyes of the toddler, they are able to take the frustration and torment out of the daily challenges of toileting, eating, sleeping, transitions, and more. But they are doing so much more beyond these day-to-day moments, whether challenging or not. They are also helping their children lay down the foundation of lifelong skills that will help them succeed. Who doesn't want their child to become kind and compassionate, resilient and resourceful, able to manage her feelings and learn to persist and stay on task when things get tough?

• Parenting Is Not One-Size-Fits-All •

So in this book, we'll be talking about a range of different ways that you can turn everyday situations into moments that set up your child for future happiness and success. It's something I live every day, both in the classroom and at home. In addition to all the children at the Toddler Center, I have three children of my own.

When I tell people that I have three children, all boys, they often respond as if they must all be alike. Nothing could be further from the truth. Although they share many similarities, including being observant and social, enjoying listening to and playing music, excelling in school, and being passionate about their interests, compassionate, and kind, in my mind they are mostly different from one another. One takes his time to warm up, sits back and observes, always has one or two close friends, and shies away from large or crowded events. Another loves to have a good time, has a large group of friends, and jumps right into new social opportunities to meet people. The third is a mix of these two. He enjoys social situations, if he knows the people well (like his two dearest friends), knows what is going to happen, who will be there, and is apprised of any changes. Otherwise, he'd rather be home in a familiar routine and around those he knows intimately—namely, his family.

All three boys are voracious readers—one taught himself to read at age four; another struggled with reading through second grade but now can't put a book down. One reads fantasy books, another devours stories about World War II and history, and another digs into the latest book series. One read all of Harry Potter three times in a year; another could not get through book one. You get the point. Readers, yes, but their taste and approach to reading are different.

I have one son who is content looking out a car or train window for hours, which makes long-distance travel a pleasure; another who can handle about an hour in a car, and then is increasingly restless. As a toddler, he would nearly lose his mind after an hour strapped in a car seat, so we know most rest stops on most highways in the East. I have one who always ate most foods, and another who ate cereal every night for dinner for nine months (seriously!) as a toddler, but eats a full array of foods now.

My oldest needed one of us to stay with him every day during the separation period at preschool, even when other parents left. Kindergarten was similar, and we had his grandfather come and stay until he was comfortable staying alone at school. Hesitant to separate at four and five, he gradually turned into a confident leader among his peers. Our second child, on the second day of preschool, turned to me and said, "You can go now. You don't have to stay. The teachers take care of us!" No issue whatsoever with separation. Same family? All boys? Yes, and yes. But they are remarkably different children, with different styles and different needs.

So what I'm saying here is this: Take the suggestions and guidelines I offer in this book, find what is useful to you and your family . . . and don't be afraid to adapt and adjust it to work best with your own little one. I think of my approach to parenting as an orientation, or as one parent said, "a set of sensibilities." That's the beauty of seeing the world through your child's eyes: it allows you to personalize your parenting style to fit what works best with your individual child, and for you. As I've watched each of my three boys grow over the past sixteen years, it becomes ever clearer to me that all children have some characteristics that stay with them for a lifetime, and others that they outgrow, or learn how to manage on their own. *Consistency* and *change* are always at play. What that means for us as parents is that we have to stay tuned into our children's unique needs at a given moment, which will be different than they were a few days or months ago.

And even though my boys are well beyond their toddler years, I am still working with toddlers every day. Between home and work, I am constantly reminded of the challenges of being a parent, and of the complexity of each child. We have to see each child for who she is—in all pieces, even the pieces we don't like or that challenge us. Usually those are pieces in our child that remind us of ourselves, the parts of self we don't like! This is the challenge.

• How This Book Works •

The book is divided into two parts. Part I focuses on understanding the developing mind of your toddler—why their behavior is so paradoxical, what's going on inside their complex (and confused) young minds, and how to use Parenting POV to get inside their heads so you can understand the world through their eyes. I've also included a chapter on what happens when we misunderstand our toddlers and inadvertently shame them and stunt their growth and developing sense of who they are. These chapters are focused on the "high-level" skills that lead to self-regulation.

Part II focuses more on "cracking the toddler code" of everyday behaviors that offer the opportunity to lay down a solid, successful foundation. I offer practical advice ("What to Do") so that you can troubleshoot day-to-day challenges that all parents face with their toddlers. You will learn how to crack the code on tantrums, sleeping, eating, toilet training, playing with peers, and more. By the end of Part II, you'll know how to use your Parenting POV in everyday moments as a way to help children develop good habits and skills not only for today, but for tomorrow as well.

Near the end of the book, you will find the Fifteen New Seeds for Success, which will help anchor you as you move through these toddler years and beyond. These Seeds echo all the lessons, advice, and examples that are woven throughout the book. They are the end result of my more than twenty years working with toddlers and their families.

As you read through the first and second parts of the book, you will find many examples from my years working with children that are intended to help you think about your own unique child (or children). It's important to keep in mind that children at this age are particularly robust, sensitive, and dynamic; they are charming, forceful, curious, loving, angry, and always engaging. But they are also quite challenging. Again, if these years are "done right," not only will the years that follow be much more harmonious for all involved but they will also lay a fertile, supportive, endlessly nurturing foundation for a child to truly flourish throughout their life—intellectually, emotionally, socially, and even physically—by letting them become the children they are meant to be. One of the hardest parts of being a parent is truly being able to step back, look at our child, try to understand *his or her* experience of the world (which is very different from our experience as adults), and remember that it is our role to *guide* them, to *support* them into becoming the person they are meant to be, so they can be happy, resourceful, resilient, determined, caring, and yes, successful in life.

part one

The Developing Mind of Your Toddler

Why They Really Do the Things They Do

When we peer into the minds and brains of toddlers, when we look underneath their often paradoxical behavior, we begin to see just how special, wonderful, needy, and vulnerable our young children are at this time in their lives. They are in the throes of mastering some of the most important skills of their lifetime; if we help them get it right now, we set them up for achievement, happiness, fulfillment, and success in all realms of their lives. Throughout the chapters in Part I, you will find vivid descriptions of what is happening in your toddler's brain and what he is grappling with developmentally, explanations of why she is behaving the way she is, and practical tips on how to shift your POV so that you can guide your child in a loving, supportive way instead of trying to control, micromanage, and inadvertently shame him.

chapter one

Setting Up Toddlers to Thrive

Self-Regulation and the Key to True Success

Why do toddlers drive parents crazy?

Maya, having just turned three, reported to her mom that she was a big girl now. She was fully toilet trained and recently moved out of the crib into her "big girl bed." The Monday after her birthday party, Maya woke up with exuberance and announced, "I can get dressed all by myself!" Unlike past mornings when she battled to get dressed or simply to pick out clothes, today she was ready to be on her own. "Go away, mommy, and I'll surprise you." Maya picked out her full outfit and got dressed—shirt, pants, socks, and even hair clips. She proudly announced this success to her family and sat down to eat breakfast, without the usual morning battle.

Her mother was thrilled and sure they had gotten past the worst of her toddler behavior. Maya chatted away, and then put some toys in her backpack, ready to head off to her toddler preschool. But it wasn't time to leave yet. Her mother suggested they read a book. Maya happily picked out a book and plopped down on her mom's lap to read. It was a calm and affectionate moment. While reading the book, they turned the page to a drawing of the book character eating pink ice cream. The mother read the words to accompany it.

As happy as ever, Maya jumped up. "I want ice cream, too!" she announced and marched toward the kitchen. Her mother kindly explained that they didn't eat ice cream in the morning, and besides, they did not have any. In mere seconds, Maya crumpled to the floor, insistent on the ice cream, now screaming and yelling, devastated that there was no pink ice cream for her.

Her mother again explained that they did not have it, but she would buy chocolate ice cream (Maya's favorite) at the store while Maya was at school.

"Nooooooo!" screamed Maya. "I need pink ice cream. Pink ice cream now!" Her mother felt helpless and frustrated as she struggled to get Maya, still flailing on the floor, in her coat and out the door for school.

What just happened? her mother wondered. *Just five minutes before we were in this lovely moment, she had dressed herself, and now she is back to that irrational, demanding baby again.*

• The Toddler Paradox: What's Going on Inside •

Toddlers: They love us, they hate us.

They seem carefree and secure one minute, playing with confidence, and afraid of their own shadows the next, fiercely clinging to our leg.

They act and speak rationally one moment and irrationally the next, screaming because we cut their bread the "wrong way."

They want to stay glued to our sides, seemingly helpless and completely dependent one day, and then push us away in fierce independence the next, yelling, "I can do it myself!"

They act like big kids one moment, feeding and dressing themselves, being polite—and then are helpless babies the next, unable to do anything for themselves.

They are laughing and full of joy one moment, and whining and in a full meltdown the next because of a simple "No."

You get the picture. Toddler behavior is often paradoxical: they seem to swing between extremes for no apparent reason—or at least, this is the way it looks to us adults. The behavior of toddlers is often mystifying, confusing, and downright challenging. Why do their moods and their actions seem so erratic and hard to predict? How can we love them with all our hearts, but feel so powerless in the face of their crazy-making behavior? The answer to these questions is found when we peek inside their brains and understand what makes toddlers tick.

• • •

Tanya was a quiet and observant two-year-old. She took her time before deciding which activity to do each day at our center and avoided being near children who were playing in a physical manner. I worked with her parents to help her feel more comfortable with her physical abilities and not be so afraid of physical play. By the end of the year, she was becoming more comfortable.

Her parents returned to see me when she was three and a half. They were confused. They described Tanya as being "a kind and sweet little girl," but now she was also "rude," they said. They didn't understand why. They reported that she had become more confident and outgoing at school and easily made friends. She tried more things on her own. She was less afraid of making mistakes. They were proud of these attributes. Then they described some recent incidents.

The mother explained, "When we get into the elevator at our apartment, Tanya is sometimes approached by a woman who asks her what her name is. Instead of answering, Tanya hides behind my leg and very loudly yells, 'I don't like you. Be quiet!' Now if we get in the elevator and she sees this woman, she does not wait for her to say anything. She just screams at her, 'I don't like you!' I am so embarrassed."

Sound like a rude behavior? From an adult point of view it is, but Tanya does not mean to be rude. More than likely, Tanya behaved the way she did because she felt like a small person in a crowded elevator. Maybe she is frightened by the woman she hardly knows, or unsure of herself, or put on the spot. All could explain her desire to not interact and instead close down the situation.

• • •

What I've observed again and again in these paradoxes is that our children often trigger well-meaning parents to try to control or fix their kids' "bad" behavior, without seeing the underlying *need* behind the behavior. I understand why this happens. A child's actual need can be hard to decipher. Toddlers often do not communicate in straightforward ways.

What children are expressing through this chaotic, turbulent way of acting is actually fairly transparent: *sometimes they feel in control of the big world they have just become a part of and are eager to explore and get to know, and sometimes they are completely overwhelmed by this same world, which can lead to feelings of anger, worry, fear, or a need for comfort.* Sometimes they are able to brush their teeth and get into bed like mom or dad has requested; other times, this request to leave their toys or the family room where mom and dad have just been sitting around the television feels like being excommunicated from the family. *Go to bed and be left all alone in that dark, scary bedroom without you? Are you kidding me?*

Children are not mini adults. They don't think like we do. They don't see the world like we see it. Toddlers are not thinking ahead of themselves. They cannot. They are beings tied amazingly to the present tense, thinking only about themselves and wanting to feel safe, loved, taken care of, and yet independent all at once.

And this is true even when toddlers seem to be acting in ways that feel adult-like: When they talk back rudely. When they walk away callously or suddenly have very specific opinions about food they will eat or clothes they will wear. Again, this behavior may confuse parents. They try to meet the child's "expressed" need or demand, but what is expressed may not really be what the child needs deeper down. And that's what we are going to do: learn to decipher toddler behavior so that you can help your child learn to manage the world on his or her own—and not through controlling their behavior but by guiding them.

Many parents who come to see me start the conversation with some variation of this question: "What happened to my darling little baby?"

So what *is* going on during the transition from being a baby to being a toddler?

As children transition from infancy to toddlerhood, they are now moving around on their own, they are talking and talking back, they suddenly have opinions, and they can refuse food, naps, and baths. They have their own desires, and when they want something, they want it *now*! Our wonderful, lovely, dependent babies vanish overnight and in their place are sometimes whiny, demanding, still-adorable imposters. Who are these little rascals who are still so cute and yet so monstrous? Who need us but don't want us? Who seem driven not by distraction but by an unstoppable inner desire to explore the world and all that is around them with their eyes, feet, hands, noses, ears, and yes, even their tongues?

When they don't behave, or they act out, or they seem to ignore our directions, we resort to certain tactics: We want them to follow our rules, be good, and behave. We cajole, beg, and bribe them with rewards. We pray and hope that by example they will model themselves after us and our good behavior. Sometimes we resort to threatening them. Or yelling at them. If we're lucky, when our toddler is really working our last nerve we can pass a child off to a babysitter or to a teacher or to a spouse and just walk away. Then, of course, our willful, strong-natured toddlers who just a minute ago didn't seem to care for us at all are suddenly blue in the face with anger and frustration. They want us! They need us! *Come baaaack!*

These scenarios probably seem familiar. Parenting a toddler sometimes feels like a battle that can't be won. Most of us have felt totally helpless in the face of our toddler at one time or another. Or maybe even many times. But it doesn't have to be like this. It may be hard to believe, but life with our toddlers can actually be calm, fun, and enjoyable. The problem is that helping our children become happy and well-adjusted in their lives does not happen because we wish it so. Nor does it happen if we try to mold them or force them into being that person we desire them to be. There is no magic trick to force kids into becoming happy, successful adults. But when we learn to accept the good and bad of what our kids express—and start to understand why the furious development, emerging sense of self, and growth in their brains are actually what's driving these dramatic swings in behavior—it all starts to make a lot more sense. You'll be able to move away from immediate judgments of the actual behavior, and instead finally be able to understand what your child is really trying to tell you. And when you know what they are communicating, the response becomes much more clear.

How the Toddler Brain Grows: Interactive, Dynamic, and Variable

As frustrating as this changeability of the toddler may be, these instances actually give us a great opportunity to get inside our kids and figure out what they are thinking and feeling and how their brain is growing at this age. We can learn to use these seemingly contradictory behaviors to understand how our children see and experience the world—and when we see the world from their vantage point, we understand who they are and what they need, putting us in a much better, calmer, and more effective position to guide them.

> Indeed, how we interact with our toddlers *now* plays an enormous role in how they develop *later*. Set a strong foundation during the toddler years, and ongoing development has a firm base. Weaken that foundation during these crucial years, and the consequences are seen for years to come.

During these years, your child is emerging as her own person, separate from you. This is an emotionally challenging process that makes the toddler years fragile, challenging, and exciting all at once, with tremendous leaps in learning and growth. But as we've been seeing, toddler behavior reflects this explosive period of growth and change. Indeed, underneath the behavior is the toddler brain—which is both malleable and vulnerable, dynamic and responsive to outside factors.

The toddler brain is not fixed by some hardwired genetic code that solely determines who children are or how they behave. All aspects of children's development—physical, emotional, social, and cognitive—are a result of the dynamic interplay between the child's biology and inherited tendencies (which include temperament) and their individual experiences (including interactions with their parents, teachers, and siblings, as well as their nutrition, opportunities for stimulation, and protection from stress). Just as it's hard to predict who will grow up to be our next president, Nobel Prize winner, or Olympic athlete, it's also hard to predict when our children will grow into their best selves. But there is one certainty: The toddler brain cannot grow or develop in the best way possible if a child is under constant stress, if he or she doesn't feel safe and secure, and if she or he is not given the kind of freedom coupled with support and limits to begin the long process of separation and individuation. Security, comfort, freedom, and limits are essential ingredients for healthy development—of the brain and the person.

Of course, every parent wants their child to grow and develop optimally, which is why psychologists and educators have been peering into the minds of young children, observing their behaviors, and analyzing their similarities and differences for centuries. Based on these scientific studies and observations, theorists have tried to define how most children grow and develop over time—as if there was some average or generalization that could be made. This line of thinking might remind you of the old debates over nature and nurture, and which is more important for development. What I can tell you is that many decades and thousands of studies demonstrate that it is a combination of the two that makes a person who they are. In fact, recent studies of the brain confirm that it's not nature versus nurture; it's nature *and* nurture. Some of what a child does is inborn, including temperament. This refers to how strongly a child reacts emotionally, how sensitive they are to noise or other distractions, how active they tend to be, how focused they can be, and how they approach new people or things. I refer to these inborn qualities as the child's *style* or *approach* in the world. But this is only one piece of the child; by no means does inborn mean destiny. Instead, those inborn qualities or tendencies are then molded and shaped by their interaction with their life experiences.

Nor does every child develop in the same way at the same time. As developmental psychologists have known for a long time, and neuroscientists are now starting to corroborate through brain research, children's development happens in response to many different factors. If it were simply about genetic makeup and hardwiring, development across children and even within one child would be remarkably consistent. And yet, no two children in a family are the same, as my own boys attest. Each child has unique needs, which in turn require different kinds of responses from us. What they all have in common is a parent who responds to their particular needs, provides ongoing guidance and comforts, and shares in the child's joys.

In other words, trying to label milestones or skills as "normal" or "typical" is so broad that it becomes useless. Take walking, for example. Pediatricians consider it within normal age range for a baby to begin walking anywhere from nine to sixteen months. That is a wide span for a basic skill. Similarly, "normal" within one child is also variable. A baby who is an early talker, speaking multiple words at ten months and sentences not long after, may not crawl until twelve months, and walk at seventeen months. Variation is the rule, not the exception.

For toddlers, indisputably the most important context for the shaping and molding within the brain is the relationship with the parents or the main caregivers raising them. Brain studies show the lasting effects of positive or negative parental care during infancy affect the offspring into adolescence and beyond: if a young child is neglected or is raised in a chronic environment of high stress (such as the emotional stress of living in poverty or the physical stress from abuse), that child's brain will be forever altered.

We also know that simply feeding and giving basic care is not enough. As clearly demonstrated by attachment studies, young children need to be held, responded to, and loved. The newer and rapidly expanding field of brain research confirms and extends this understanding, reinforcing just how crucial this early caregiver interaction is to the healthy development of a child—cognitively, emotionally, and socially—and underscoring the damages and long-term consequences of not having a positive caregiver-infant relationship. These basic needs for love, nurturance, and care must be met for a child to thrive. If any or all are absent, a child's brain architecture will literally develop a different pathway, one that can hijack a child's ability to grow and learn to his or her full potential throughout life.

The bottom line is this: Early experience matters and early caregiving relationships matter a lot. This is probably no surprise to you. Most parents recognize this importance. But what is often not made clear to us in the throes of this turbulent time is *how* to interact with our young children. How should we provide them with the love and comfort they need? To help them feel understood, and at the same time provide boundaries to give them the structure they need to navigate this stage of life? The answers to these crucial questions are about balance—a balance between giving them the room to move on their own and providing them with limits. Overly controlling a child this age can be damaging long past the toddler years, but so is a free-for-all without rules and limits. When you understand the world through your child's eyes, seeing their unique needs gets easier, and so does giving the response that fits and provides the optimal balance.

The toddler years set into place the grounding children require for healthy lifelong fulfillment, achievement, and success. But it is not always a smooth ride, as any parent or caregiver knows.

• Self-Regulation Is the Key •

Toddlers are in the throes of many new and complex emotions (anger, fear, worry, sadness, elation, pride, shame) and making new neural connections every day (through their senses, through language, through their play). And often toddlers don't quite know how to handle all this new information and stimulation. Their thoughts, feelings, and responses hit them intensely. This is why toddlers throw themselves on the floor in hysterics, or unexpectedly go from happy to angry or sad within seconds. They can't yet control the rapidly shifting feelings that all this new information triggers inside them. And this is all totally normal.

But what toddlers are also starting to learn (albeit slowly and somewhat painfully) is a set of emotional and cognitive skills or processes that come together under the umbrella called self-regulation. It is a term you may have heard or read about in the media. Developmental psychologists have studied this for decades. Neuroscientists are investigating it closely. There is a reason for so much focus on it. Self-regulation is what enables a child to handle intense thoughts and emotions, keep on task, bounce back from a disappointment, solve problems, listen to his parents or teachers, make friends, manage everyday stress, and develop the coping mechanisms to do so. Self-regulation skills are a mix of social, emotional, and cognitive (thinking) skills—I refer to them as key life skills—that enable kids to navigate both their inner world of thoughts and feelings and the world around them. Self-regulation skills are consistently tied to lifelong success in academics, physical and mental health, personal relationships, and overall quality of life. These skills are among the core aspects of what is referred to as "executive function." And though children don't learn or master these skills all at once, or even completely until later in life (during late adolescence), the toddler years provide an amazing opportunity to lay their foundation.

These life skills enable a child to calm herself down, communicate what she needs, and stay relatively secure throughout the day, even during times of change and transition. (For more on transitions, see chapter 7.) As the child gets older, these skills are essential and allow him to make good decisions, handle hard situations, focus attention, problem solve, and override inappropriate actions (such as wanting to hit someone when angry, or thrusting a toy across the room because the desire is there).

For the sake of being clear, there are two ways to think about how toddlers develop these crucial self-regulatory skills: first, their brains are hardwired to do so, if the conditions are good enough; and second, we, their parents, caregivers, teachers, and guardians, help them to develop these skills through modeling, guiding, providing comfort, and scaffolding. Developing self-regulation skills takes repeated practice over time, and much parental guidance is required. In other words, we are a big part of how kids learn to self-regulate.

• Self-Regulation in the Brain •

Let's first take a look at what's happening with the toddler brain. As toddlers emerge from infancy, their brains are just beginning to develop the structures that manage vitally important functions. While neuroscience on this stage of development is new and growing each year, there is still much to be learned. Nonetheless, we have a basic understanding of some of the pieces that make the toddler years both critical for lifetime well being and success and at the same time challenging to parents or adults who care for young children.

It is important to understand that there are three "processing centers" in the brain, and they are all interconnected and yet distinct. At the bottom of the brain is the area that controls breathing, heartbeat, and other automatic functions: the things that keep us alive. The middle section of the brain is the emotional center. All sensations and experiences travel through this part before going to our highest, thinking level of the brain, the cortex. It is important to know that the two lower centers of our brain are wired much earlier and more completely than our cortex. They also fire much faster. So all of us experience our emotions long before our reasoning kicks in. But for toddlers this difference is even more dramatic.

Toddlers often feel the full force of an emotional response

without having the ability to rationally "think" their way out of it. Through the toddler years, connections are being made between the higher level of the brain and the emotional centers. In fact, this is the most important learning and wiring occurring in toddler brain development. But connections take years (many!) to create and become automatic. This network develops over many, many life events. This linking between thinking and emotion happens in the hundreds of small interactions your child has with you and other important people every single day. Every time you comfort your child or walk them through a routine, you are helping form these connections.

As parents, we can want to hurry up this process, looking forward to calmer times. But learning simply takes time. Do you ever wonder why you have to repeat the same routine every day ("first socks, then shoes"), maybe even several times in a day? It is because these connections are forming but are not yet complete. Think back to the last time you learned a difficult and complex task (golf, knitting, making a soufflé). It took several or even many trials before you became proficient. And some days, that skill seems to suddenly disappear (how did you land in that sand trap after all this time?).

The same is true with toddlers. They need to experience events over and over (and over!) again to master them, especially something as hard as managing strong emotions. Lots of practice and repetition are needed. Every time you respond to a frightened child with comforting words, "Oh . . . that was scary. The noise was so loud. I'm here with you. You're safe," or you encourage your child to persist in a task by labeling their feelings, "You're feeling so frustrated because that puzzle piece doesn't fit! You can try again and it might fit," your child is building connections between thoughts, feelings, and soothing. Over hundreds or even thousands of trials, your child will begin to internalize this process. She'll start to say to herself, "This is hard but I can do it," or your son will say, "It's scary but I'm okay." Children learn to use their thoughts and words to manage feelings and organize their behavior based on these many interactions with you over time. ("Hitting people hurts. But I can hit that hammer toy instead.") And it's this ability to cope with strong feelings and handle behavior in socially acceptable ways that is the essence of self-regulation, which is also one of the best predictors of achievement and well-being throughout the life span (more on that later in chapter 8).

At the brain level, the prefrontal cortex (that part of the brain's architecture that supports regulation and the main executive functions) is very much still developing at birth and even well through adolescence and into early adulthood. The infant is fully dependent on the caregiver to calm them and help them regulate. Toddlers, thanks to a combination of these gradually developing structures in the frontal lobe, coupled with their growing desire for independence, start to handle life a bit more on their own—but they still rely on us. As a parent, you know this, because children, at around age two, first push back with their own ideas and preferences with a mind of their own. The difficulty arises because toddlers have their own ideas at a time when these brain structures are only beginning to develop; they still have a long way to go before they will be fully on board and useful. Which is why toddlers do not yet have a well-developed brain capacity for thinking through situations, for controlling emotions or behavior, for acting "politely" or stopping behaviors they should not be doing, for making decisions or knowing what is right or wrong. Yet. These abilities are a work in progress—and they will, with proper support and attention from us, improve as the brain matures. At this point in time, you, the parent, act as their organizer and regulator. Later, the child will be able to do it for themselves. Did I mention that toddlers and teenagers have a lot in common?

The grounding for self-regulation and executive function begins to be laid starting with the earliest caregiver-infant interactions. The comforting and calming that parents provide for their infants is thought to build these brain structures. Think back to infancy. When our children were infants, we knew they needed our help calming down. We swaddled our newborns; we held, rocked, and comforted them. We relied on routines to help them settle in at night and wake up in the morning. We knew in a commonsense way that babies need food and sleep to grow.

But when our babies become toddlers, we automatically begin to interact with them in a different way: we begin to take

Toddlers Need to Make Mistakes . . . and We Need to Let Them

Toddlers' modus operandi is to test themselves and figure out how to do tasks on their own. They learn by making mistakes, over and over, and trying again. This is part of figuring out who they are. But if they see an attempt as a mistake, if they think they have failed, they don't keep trying. They give up. When we as parents insist there is always a "right way," we take away the opportunity for our children to exercise independence and learn from mistakes. We also tell them that their way is wrong. Correcting a child is the same as controlling him, and both correcting and controlling rob your child of the chance to prove that he is growing. That's what he wants you to see and acknowledge. That's how he figures out what he can do. Toddlers are all about learning through their mistakes, through trial and error, regardless of the outcome. And when you support his explorations and share in his delights, he feels valued and safe.

a step back and often take away some of the care and attention. This makes sense: it's our hardwired human instinct to help the toddler on her path toward becoming independent. But what we need to keep in mind is that even though they are acting like they want independence (which they do!), they need us just as strongly as they did when they were babies, just in a new and different, and sometimes quite intense, way.

• Giving Your Child the Skills to Thrive •

Ask any parent what he or she wants most for their children and the majority will say, "I want my child to be happy." Yes, parents also want their kids to be safe and resilient, knowing the world can be an adversarial place and that in order to truly succeed in life—in whatever they aspire to do and be—they need to develop certain emotional skills and become well-adjusted. They will also say they want their children to be "kind," "caring," "respectful," and often "successful" and "smart." These are all values that most of us share. Who wouldn't want a child to grow up to be kind, caring, successful, and happy?

But can we really *make* our children happy? Can we force them to be genuinely kind?

No. We really can't make our kids do anything. We can kiss them, love them, hug them, and indulge them. We can sign them up for myriad activities, plan playdates and vacations, give them music lessons, Mandarin classes, gymnastics, soccer, and ballet, and do our utmost to get them into the best schools.

But think about it for a moment—is "happiness" really what we are after anyway?

This drive we have as happy-seeking, often overachieving parents begins early—our plump little babies are allowed to coo, cry, spit up, and awaken us at night until they are about one year and ten months. Then, whammo! As soon as they reach two years old, suddenly and as if overnight, we have a whole new set of rules for them: we want them to behave, listen, follow rules, and "be nice." And just as we shift our expectations of our no-longer babies, all hell seems to break loose. A switch is flicked and our sweet little ones turn into demanding, irrational, often defiant toddlers. We worry that if we don't clamp down on their "bad" behaviors now, they will have these behaviors forever.

It may surprise you to know that parents often—unwittingly, unintentionally—get in the way of their toddlers growing into the well-adjusted, empathetic, resilient, happy older children and adults they envision them to be. Parents often think they are doing what is best for their children, when in fact, all they are doing is blocking the needs that are at the core of who that child is. And when we suffocate those needs, or even simply overlook them, when we, unwittingly or not, try to mold our children, and shape their behavior according to some preconceived expectations of who they are and who we think they ought to be, we stamp out and smother them. We deny them the crucial foundation necessary for every child to grow up well. By getting in their way (we'll explore the ways we can inadvertently sabotage our children's development in chapter 4), we take away their ability to understand themselves, to explore the world in a way that makes sense to them and encourages their curiosity. We truncate their motivation to learn. We take away their confidence to forge relationships, and most crucial of all, we interrupt their ability to develop the emotional skills necessary for them to succeed in school and in life.

I don't mean succeed in the way we tend to think of success these days: that they will become straight-A students, awesome athletes, accomplished artists, or the next great business innovators—though all of that might happen, too. What I mean by success is this: a person who feels confident to explore the world around him with excitement and curiosity, who is not afraid to make mistakes, who feels secure enough to begin to make friends, and who feels well-adjusted enough to bounce back when she is disappointed. A person who can handle life is motivated to learn, stands up for herself, and cares about others. Sound too good to be true?

Not at all.

Toddlers do or say many things that from an adult point of view appear to be irrational, unsocialized, or even absurd. Indeed, many of our toddlers' seemingly illogical choices make us parents very nervous. We can get embarrassed. Our response? We tend to overcorrect them, or criticize them, or simply stop them. As adults, we see our toddlers' erratic behavior as needing to be controlled because they seem so out of control, which, from an adult view, they might be. This is when we tend to fall back on generalizations about the classic "terrible twos"—or threes or fours. We see kids this age as misbehaving or rude or not listening or losing it or throwing temper tantrums over nothing. But when looked at with fresh eyes, these misbehaviors can make sense, even to us. Then you will be able to guide your child through it to a more socialized way of being. Eventually.

• • •

So what can parents do? There are six key ways parents can interact with their toddler. Parents can:

1. mirror back a sense of safety and relative order;
2. listen to children instead of always talking at and directing them;
3. give children freedom to play and explore on their own;

4. allow children the space and opportunity to struggle and fail;
5. work to understand who each individual child is and what he needs at a given age; and
6. provide children with limits, boundaries, and guidance.

These simple actions (which I will expand upon in later chapters) give any child a strong foundation to grow during a time when they are just beginning to test and understand themselves in relation to others and respond to and manage their complicated feelings.

And guess what happens when we interact with our kids in this way? We suddenly become disentangled from the battles; calm and clear enough to respond to what our child is really needing at any given moment (rather than starting with what the adult needs at that moment); and flexible enough to give our kids choices while at the same time providing support and boundaries.

My approach is a child-centered way of guiding kids safely and confidently, stimulating their minds and imaginations and motivating them to develop a strong sense of self and meaningful relationships to others. By parenting in this way, we give our children the opportunity to be curious, creative, resilient, and, yes, happy; a recipe for lifelong success. At the same time, it's up to us as parents to provide a road map and set boundaries and limits. By shifting your perspective and learning to see the world through the eyes of your child, the way you parent will change, enabling your children to be and become who they are meant to be.

This is not a boilerplate guide that offers one, two, three steps to discipline and manage your child. It's not a set of rules to follow that promise that your child will be well behaved, well regulated, and end up happy. At the end of the day, any attempt to proscribe children's behavior based on desired outcome will likely fail. Instead, my approach is about shifting your point of view—showing you how to look at the world through your toddler's eyes so that you can understand your child's needs more clearly and accurately. Your child, in turn and over time, begins to learn how to meet these needs for themselves, always with your support. When a child's essential needs are taken care of (and we'll see what needs are indeed essential and which are not), you not only lay down the emotional and psychological foundation that enables your child's fullest potential but you also feel much more fulfilled and happy as a parent. The two go hand in hand.

Although not tied to a prescription (because no one-size prescription can fit every child as if they are all the same), my approach does offer a practical framework and set of strategies that will not only give you a stronger sense of flexibility and options about how to help your children calm down or move through transitions, for example, but will also position you to direct your children more kindly and gently, in ways that kids can actually benefit from. With this kind of parenting, kids flourish because they begin to understand the different feelings they have, internalize self-regulatory skills, make choices and decisions, understand consequences of their actions, and understand who they are and how they relate to others. In short, they become able to manage their own behavior and learn how to handle life. And according to the latest findings in neuroscience and psychology, these skills form the basis of lifelong success, ranging from school achievement to friendships to being empathic, creative, and innovative.

You may be thinking, *So what does this shift in perspective look like?* Hearing directly from parents will best illustrate this shift. As one parent said to me, "Helena was about to go into a tailspin about what she was wearing; if I reacted to her by yelling at her, or getting upset that she couldn't decide, or wouldn't get dressed, then she would get more upset. But I now understand how hard this seemingly simple request can be for her. So, if I don't react, and give her some time to work through her indecision, she usually calms down. The moment passes and we move on."

Another noted, "I was so worried about my child being weak and whiney. There was so much he could not do and I worried there was something wrong. But since you helped me see that I had to trust him to do more for himself, and that he actually *wanted* to do more, he is so much better. In two weeks, I have let go and let him make mistakes. He is so much happier and feels so good about himself!"

Parents have to learn to trust themselves as they make this shift in perspective and begin to see the world from their toddler's point of view. At first it may feel awkward, even uncomfortable. But when you cue in to your child, and check your own response to a certain situation, you will begin to see underneath your child's behavior and understand what she or he really needs. And then remarkable things happen. Parents stay calm and confident, and kids slowly but surely learn how to navigate their own feelings, make decisions, and trust themselves—yes, at two, three, four, and five years old.

In some ways, this book is a gentle reminder of what many of you probably already, intuitively know: how to parent in a way that enables your child to become that kind, compassionate, motivated, curious, well-adjusted, and happy person you envision. Parenting not from the point of view of trying to manage or control their behaviors with hopes that they turn out how you wish for them to be. Parenting, instead, is about understanding the unique person your child is—one who is in an intense, not quite predictable, state of emergence and flux, especially at the prime ages of two to five. And this means both guiding them through the day-to-day challenges of eating, handling tantrums, getting dressed, and getting along with friends while helping them build the lifelong skills needed to become a well-regulated, competent, and caring person who can handle life with all its ups and downs.

chapter two

The Toddler Paradox

Why They Pull You Close and Then Push You Away

Xavier, age three, burst into the classroom one day, exuberant and angry. He wore a cape and announced that he was Superman. He marched around the room for much of the session with a scowl on his face and announced to the teachers that he was mad. At one point, he was a dinosaur, crushing things with his feet; at another point, he tried to throw objects around the room. He announced that he did not want to play with anyone today, that he was a "strong boy and no one can get near me."

When I spoke with the mother, she reported that at home he also was being Superman and expressing a lot more anger. She could not figure out why. The mother had started a new job recently after being at home, but several months had passed. We wondered together if Xavier's behavior was a reaction to her being at work each day. But then she revealed something else: "He has been missing his cousin who he plays with twice a week. He goes over to his grandmother's and plays with her there. But not for the past few weeks."

"Why?" I asked.

The mother explained that his grandmother was away, traveling with the cousin and her family for a month.

I figured we had hit it. Not only was his cousin away, but his grandmother was with them. Could he be jealous? I went on the assumption that he was. His anger and need to be in control by wearing the cape and being Superman made sense. It was a response to his jealousy and confusion. *Where had grandma gone? And why did she take my cousin and not me?*

That day at school, we gave him outlets to express his anger over his grandma's being away, and missing her. We validated his feelings, reminded him it was not his fault that grandma was away, and reinforced that she would be back soon. His relief (and release) was evident on his face, in his body, and through his lighter, but still empowered, Superman play. Soon he started talking about mommy being at work. Whereas she used to pick him up after school, now their neighbor did. Finally, he collapsed in tears into a teacher's arms for comfort, crying, "I miss Mommy."

The erratic, seemingly paradoxical behavior of toddlers is normal and to be expected: children are expressing their emotions in the only way they can at this age, still limited by their developing verbal capabilities and minimal knowledge of feelings. They are caught between two battling needs: the desire for self and independence versus the need for comfort, security, and the familiar—in other words, mama or dada. In the case of Xavier, he projected feeling big and strong and wanting to be apart from others, when in fact, inside, he was sad, angry, confused, and needing to be close for comfort.

The Toddler: Exploration Phase

The exploration phase begins when the young toddler starts to walk. By eighteen months, and continuing over the next few years, your child is on a nearly nonstop adventure of discovery, combined with growing abilities—physical skills (for example, climbing, running, throwing), fine motor skills (for example, eating with utensils, drawing, zipping coat), language skills (from words to sentences, more complex ideas, then stories), social skills (such as playing with peers in increasingly sophisticated ways), and the ability to handle emotions. No wonder your toddler gets exhausted, breaks down, and needs your support and comfort. Even older children, beyond five, reach this point sometimes.

In the early stages of this physical mobility, up to about age three, he is also beginning to use language—a reflection of the enormous cognitive changes going on in his brain. Between the ages of two and five there will be enormous changes in their language abilities, which ties into their ability to communicate with others, to understand emotions, to be empathic, and to engage in pretend play. These areas all overlap.

As toddlers learn to speak, they are not simply labeling objects or saying words; they are trying to communicate their needs, but often ineffectively. Language allows children to communicate, but not always in a direct way, or in a way that makes sense to adults.

With the leaps in language development come new ways of thinking and growing physical capabilities. What does this mean? A push for more autonomy, to do more "by myself," to try out more new things. And for this reason, parents need to establish clear limits. Limits make it safe for the toddler to explore.

All kids have negative emotions and should have negative emotions. And when they reach some kind of limit or extreme, children at this age will lose it and feel pushed too far. They may even act out. Have meltdowns. Or get sullen and whiney. All of these responses are completely normal, and more to the point, healthy. For parents, this situation means understanding what's going on inside the toddler mind and brain. You have to look under the behavior and decipher what your child *really* needs at this time in his or her life.

• Pulling Us Close, Pushing Us Away: A Closer Look •

At an emotional and social level, toddlers' primary needs are defined by two instinctual drives that explain most if not all of their behavior: the need to separate and the accompanying desire to become an independent being with a sense of self. Both of these drives begin in their relationship with you.

Our children are born dependent on us. Newborns come into the world wanting and needing to feel loved and cared for and to become attached. Their brains are wired for this attachment relationship. You may have read about attachment. There are many thousands of studies over the past thirty years that have examined parent-child attachment and established why the interactions in this first relationship are so important, particularly with mothers or the primary caregiver. Attachment is that first or primary relationship, usually with parents, that forms over the first year of life. Based on the many interactions between the baby and parent, the many times the parent responds to the infant's needs, every day, over the first year of life, an important bond is formed between parent and child. When the relationship involves a back-and-forth between an infant who has needs and a parent who provides responsive and sensitive comfort and care, and shares the enjoyment of being their parent (at least most of the time!), the infant is able to form a sense of security and trust that others will take care of him. These trusting feelings eventually become a core for their sense of self. Equally important is that the infant develops feelings that she deserves to be loved and cared for.

It is this early relationship that sets the child up to develop competently, now and in the future. In fact, this first relationship is so important that it sets up success in how children think, handle emotions, relate and make friends, develop empathy and caring, and do well in school. Studies have begun to map how these early attachment relationships are encoded in the brain and either help (secure attachment) or hinder (insecure attachment, or neglect/chronic trauma) brain development. The tracks laid down in the brain during the early years are so important that they affect development long past these early ages. This clearly shows how much parenting during the infant and toddler years matters. It matters a lot.

All babies become attached, even if it is a challenging infant who fusses a lot, or if it takes a while before you feel like you are in rhythm with your baby. Over time, and through many occasions of comfort and care, you and your baby work out your unique relationship. Then quite suddenly, after our babies enter the second year of life and as soon as they become upright and mobile, their entire world opens up and they want and need to begin exploring that world around them and who they are in it. And this big departure from being held, swaddled, and fed means they have to be given some freedom. But here's the thing parents can overlook: they still need us. Plain and simple as that. They still need our love, our caring for them, and our ways of keeping them safe. The world, which is so exciting to explore and such a big place, is also filled with uncertainty, newness, and fear! That is why our relationships with our children at this age are crucial. They also are complicated, often stressful, and even quite volatile.

Therein lies the irony of the first two years of life: the baby must become attached in order to move away and separate. First, when she is safe in your arms, it is your gentle, loving care and meeting her needs that helps her gain the required sense of security. And then, after they feel secure that you are there for them, it is this feeling of safety and trust that motivates them to let go and successfully move away from you as soon as they become a toddler.

As we've seen, the changes in their brain during this time are rapid, and the brain structures for controlling and handling emotions and thoughtful planning are quite new and not anywhere close to fully developed. So what does this mean for our toddlers? They really cannot manage intense or negative emotions too well (yet), and stopping themselves from doing something they should not is equally hard at this age. These are the self-regulation skills, or life skills, we discussed in the last chapter. The drives for separation and self, coupled with emerging brain development, are what underlie much of what young children do: when they try to control their impulses, explode in anger, melt down, refuse to go to sleep, or try to get along with other kids. It's what's behind their difficulty getting dressed in the morning, getting out the door at any time, sitting at the dinner table, being quiet in a library, or learning how to become increasingly independent even when they need your help.

As if this mind-brain situation weren't complicated enough, these drives meet head-on with the child's realization that he can't be totally on his own—nor does he want to be. At times he may act like he is ready for full independence, but he'll also realize quickly that there are so many things he can't do without you—from tying his shoes to falling asleep on his own. In the end, they don't really want to be alone anyhow; rather, they want to be left alone to try things for themselves. With you close by. That is the crux of the challenge—to be independent but not alone. You can see why this age is complicated and confusing—to them and to us. Children this age truly fear being left alone. This deep need to stay attached is as intense as the need to separate. So, in many ways, they need us more now than ever.

I call these daily struggles for independence yet closeness the "push and pull" dynamic of toddlers; these moments reflect the storminess and turbulence of behaviors, feelings, and states of mind of children between the ages of two and five. Children at these ages embody this push-pull so much that it becomes the larger context for their lives at this time. Yet their ways of showing or expressing this push-pull conflict vary, from being quiet and keeping much of it inside to showing it more outwardly in lots of paradoxical and confusing ways (at least to adults).

This push-pull between separating and becoming independent, coupled with a profound need for a safe, familiar place to return for comfort, leads to great emotional upheaval and the back-and-forth behaviors at this age. When parents understand how these two developmental challenges affect everything about their toddler's world, suddenly their children seem a lot less mysterious. The child who can't wait to go to playgroup one week and the next throws a tantrum at home when it is time to get ready to leave for playgroup, refusing to put on his jacket and shoes, is trying to sort through his mixed feelings: *leaving home, which I know so well, is always hard even though I like playgroup.*

One day they like bananas, and the next they are repelled to their core, screaming, "You know I hate bananas!" Meanwhile, the parent is thinking, *What is wrong with you? You ate bananas yesterday and now you are saying you don't like them? That is utterly ridiculous!*

The child who likes bananas one day and hates them the next is figuring out his own preferences and testing out his power: *Do I listen to Mommy or am I my own boss? Do I really like bananas, or do I eat them because Mommy says to?*

Remember Maya from the previous chapter, who wanted pink ice cream? She was ready to be a big girl one moment, and the very next, with a trigger that no one could have predicted, she seemed to regress into her former, little girl self. Inside she is struggling. *I want to be a big girl. Am I ready to be a big girl? Am I still little? I still need the comforts of being little.*

Keep in mind, too, that while this intense push-pull, which activates many emotions, is happening, children have to handle this storminess with a brain that is not fully capable of managing emotions well. In a way, you can see their behaviors as the result of dueling needs:

- They want to be separate from you, but also stay attached.
- They want to be independent and dependent.
- They are freedom seeking, but also need limits and structure in order to feel safe.

These dueling needs can lead to dueling behaviors and feelings:

- They feel loving toward you, as well as hateful or rageful.
- They can be polite, and equally rude.
- They can seem sensitive to others as well as completely self-absorbed.

- They can be risky and courageous as well as overly cautious and timid.
- They can act like a big kid, and then like a baby or younger version of themselves.

Toddlers at their core are nearly possessed by a burning desire to be their own person (Me!), developing their own wishes, ideas, likes, and dislikes. As they separate and develop into being their own person, they are also developing desires (often different from yours) and a sense of self. In other words, they want what they want. And what you, the parent, intends for them can be seen as an intrusion or roadblock.

The conflict that arises for the toddler is this: at the very same time they need to be certain that you, the beloved parent, are the rock that will never leave their side. Can you see the head-on push-pull unfolding? The push is an irresistible drive forward to go out in the world and become their own person. The equally intense pull is back to the comfort of the familiar, the person they know best and trust, who provides comfort and security. Push-pull; over and over again. But the parent who is often on the receiving end of all this conflicted behavior cannot always stay calm and keep on course when their child keeps pushing them away, battling them, ignoring them and then screaming for them to come closer! But don't be fooled. As she begins to separate, she needs you close by to pick her up when she falls or needs comfort. This is why it's also so crucial for parents to tune in and pay attention to their child's point of view at this time.

Here's the paradox again: Toddlers, as we are seeing, may look like they need less of our comfort and direction, when in fact the opposite is true. They are still very fragile and in need of our protection and support. Providing them with cues, guidance, boundaries, and comfort is an absolute necessity, especially as they become more autonomous.

• Practicing Their Independence •

Separation, of course, does not happen all at once. It's an evolving process with lots of back-and-forth movement. At the same time that your child wants and needs to separate from you to explore the world with his hands, feet, eyes, ears, and tongue, he also needs you—your comfort and protection as well as guidance and limits. The child wants to be her own person but equally wants to know you are taking care of her. Imagine two opposing goals fully in effect at once—wanting to be apart and wanting to be together. Seem difficult? It can be. So it is no wonder it can drive a parent, or any rational adult, crazy. Only when we begin to think about the world through the eyes of our young children does it start to make sense.

One day the child feels big. As one three-and-a-half-year-old demanded: "When do *I* get to be a grown-up? I want to be a grown-up now!" The next day she feels little. This same child battled meal and bedtime for the next week, sleeping one night in her ballerina tutu and new backpack, a clear reminder of her age. In her quest to be "grown up" she asserted herself in the only way she knew. Big and little, the motto of the toddler years.

As parents, we go through our own conflict: part of us wants that child to grow up and grow up fast so that the land of hiccups, control battles, and tantrums will be left behind (ask parents of teens about revisiting this again!). But another part of us wants to hold on to that baby forever. We are not always aware of these feelings. As you get more familiar both with what your child is thinking and feeling and what *you* are thinking and feeling about your child's development, guiding your child will become simpler and smoother. You will be seeing your child's needs through his or her eyes—as if for the first time.

This constant shifting from needing the parent to wanting to be out on their own can be confusing for parents, too. Some parents might experience a sense of relief or excitement; other parents might feel uncomfortable, sad, nervous or afraid, even angry, or a confusing combination of all these emotions. Just as their children are vacillating between intense extremes of emotion, so too are parents.

When young children vacillate in their behavior—pushing us away and pulling us toward them—they are practicing what it feels like to be independent. They push us away so they can begin to internalize the sense that they are their own person. As one father tried to help his three-and-a-half-year-old daughter put on her coat, she reprimanded him loudly and snatched the coat out of his hand. "Let me do this myself! I am gonna be four!"

But as soon as children demand their independence, they just as quickly get the feeling they need to be grounded again, with a desire for our reassurance and comfort. This leads to battles and internal struggles for parents—*Does he need me or doesn't he?*—and often parental frustration.

In the next minute or hour after they demand to do it their own way without your help, when they are climbing onto your lap at the end of a long day, or breaking down into tears as soon as they walk through the door after school, they are showing you that they've worked hard all day being a "big kid" but now they really, really need you. Inside, they are still little, needy, and fragile. This again is the constant push-pull of the two- to five-year-old. *They need to be reminded again and again that when they need you, you really are there for them.* It may sound odd, but the more they try things on their own and venture out to explore the world, the more intense their need for you becomes. And each time they feel comforted again by you, it is practice for life; they internalize the understanding that "no matter how hard things get, no matter how angry or upset I feel, or how much I push Mommy or Daddy away, they are still there for me. I am not alone."

But as we know, life is not perfect. There are always days and moments when our children need us as touchstones, and we are particularly exhausted or impatient. Maybe your toddler has challenged you over and over all day, or you have finished a long day yourself, and the toddler's meltdown is the last straw. Instead of letting him climb into your lap for comfort and reconnecting or listening patiently to his tear-filled cries, you snap. Or you criticize him. Or you tell him to be quiet or stop crying.

This happens. There is no perfect parent. We are all human. What's crucial for parents to see and understand is that during the toddler years, the needs of the child (for autonomy and exploration, coupled with support and comfort) and the needs of the parent (for time for self, or the need for the child to be good) come into constant misalignment. As we saw, when children are infants, parents have little problem deferring to the needs of the infant. But as the toddler grows, parents tend to put more pressure on the toddler to conform, to be "good"—when they help their children learn to become toilet trained, give up the bottle and the pacifier, and to speak nicely. The desires of parent and toddler have to be renegotiated as needs change, and the toddlers themselves need explicit help moving out of the comforts of being a baby into the exciting but as yet unknown benefits of growing up and being independent. But the desire to see the world (if the toddler is healthy) is natural and unstoppable. The pull is simply exhilarating. And as exciting as that is, it is also frightening. Even exhausting. Be careful what you wish for! This is where tantrums and refusals come in.

For parents, this can be equally exhausting and daunting. A child in hysterics because you put his boots on him to get out the door in a timely fashion when he wanted to do it himself (in spite of his dallying and not doing it) can be downright maddening. Sometimes you handle it well; sometimes you don't. It may sound odd, but the mishap is not the problem, so long as there is a positive reconnection, a repair. The key at times like these—when their needs collide with ours—is how you reconnect with your child. Coming back together again, without blame (which I will explain in chapter 6), lets them know you are here for them, always, even when bad moments happen. Children need to feel this deep trust, to feel you will take care of them, in bad times and good. Otherwise there is too much risk in exploring, moving out, or taking chances of any kind. This is all part of the shift in point of view that will begin to reshape your interaction with your child.

In fact, I see the needs of the parent and child collide all the time. A frequent reason parents come to see me is sleep issues. It is common for parents to say that they took their two- or two-and-a-half-year-old out of the crib because "I thought she was ready," or "He seemed so big for it," and now the child won't stay in her bed. This is one example of the parent's desire for the child to be bigger, before she is up to the task. Similarly, I have met with parents who told me that their child always fell asleep fine with his pacifier. At age three, even though sleep was the only time he used it, they decided he was old enough to fall asleep on his own—after all, "He is three"—so they suddenly took it away. The reason they came to see me? The child no longer goes to sleep at a reasonable time and wakes up repeatedly at night. He was used to his comfort; the parents were ready to move on. The issue here is not the pacifier. It is the clash of parent's and child's needs at that moment.

Another example is a four-year-old who was throwing tantrums worse than the parents had ever seen. They were leaving in a few weeks to visit relatives overseas. They had prepared

A Toddler's-Eye View of the World

Seeing the world through the eyes and mind of your toddler means repeatedly reminding your children, in your words and actions, that they are not alone, that you (their secure base) are there for them when needed. During this time, it is the parent who has to keep reminding them that they have that base to return to. What do we mean by secure base? It is the positive and calming feeling the child carries with them when they go out in the world to explore—that they can always come back to the parent for love, comfort, and reassurance. Even if the parent is not close by, the child feels they are not alone. You are their "home base." These feelings of security, of "I am okay, even if I fall," of knowing that if they make mistakes, or get scared, or just need a little comfort, you will be there, result from a relationship where a reliable parent (or caregiver) responds lovingly to their needs and watches out for them.

The young child develops an internalized sense of a secure base through you and because of you. Only then can they develop a deep belief in their own competence, that they will be okay, and have the courage and curiosity to venture further out in the world. With you helping them form this internal secure base, children can try new things, make mistakes, and recover.

their son for weeks by talking about the trip and the people he would see. On his own, this eager little boy who liked things organized packed a backpack with books and toys he wanted on the airplane, seemingly excited about the trip. I suggested to the parents that they were talking too much about the trip, because two weeks was still far away for him. They assured me, "He knows about time and he likes being prepared far in advance."

Nonetheless, the tantrums worsened and the smallest requests set up monumental meltdowns, until one day the mother asked if he was worried about the trip.

"Yes," Conrad quietly confirmed.

"Why are you upset about it?" his mother asked in surprise. "We will see Grandma and your cousins."

Conrad, now teary-eyed, continued: "Because I don't want to get so small. I'm scared."

Perplexed, the mother could not figure this out until Conrad stated, "When the plane goes up in the sky it gets small. I don't want to be small likc that. You won't be able to see me," and he started to cry. Big? Maybe. But he still thinks like a little boy. And that is the part we need to remember.

• What's Unique About Your Child •

All of the changes and needs at this age may sound complicated. In unpacking the puzzle of understanding children from two to five, there is one more piece. Mixed in with the incredible growth that occurs is the large range of variation from one child to the next. Clearly, all children are different. But before we turn to what is unique in your own child, let's first look at what is similar across children. Besides what is happening inside the mind of a young child as she figures out "me," there are broadly congruent patterns across children's behavior and how they express themselves, move, grow, and learn at these ages. These patterns give us a sense of what is considered typical at a given age. Yet even within these patterns, they are all different people, and no two children follow exactly the same pattern. This is individual variability. So, why is this variability important to keep in mind for us as parents and caregivers? In this day and age of hyperfocus on our children, with vast amounts of information available (for better or worse), parents often find themselves comparing and contrasting their children with other kids. "My child walked at ten months." "My daughter was speaking in full sentences at two years old." "My son Henry argues with me at three!" "Sophia is still not talking and she's three and a half. Is something wrong?" "Our oldest child learned to read at four and now his sister is almost five and shows no interest in letters. What's the matter?"

Parents wonder. Parents worry. I find that parents worry more than in the past. They want to know ultimately that their children are healthy and will succeed in life. Sometimes they want to know if they are "normal." All of these questions and impulses to compare our children are perfectly understandable, but I cannot emphasize enough that you need to keep in mind that children all vary—they grow at different rates, they express themselves in different ways, they show strengths and weaknesses in different areas and different contexts. Remember how you'd hear that baby Charlotte could sleep through the noise of her four brothers running around the house but that quiet Ben would wake from a nap at the sound of a pin drop? No child is perfectly even and skills don't come "on line" all at the same time. Our kids are different from one another, and that is what makes each one the special person he or she is. They differ even within themselves, changing in certain situations or contexts. A child may behave one way in one situation and the polar opposite a day later.

Every child has her own unique style, and that is important for parents to recognize. Sometimes we love and embrace parts of this unique style; other times we get worried or confused by our child's unique manner. How your child approaches new situations, moves in the world, explores, responds to change, shows emotions, and takes in people and information is part of his approach. Every child handles the world in his own way, even though there are commonalities across children this age (there is that variability again!). Understanding how your child views the world is a combination of understanding this stage of development and knowing your child's approach in the world.

The questions below are designed to help you think about your own child's approach to life. They will help tease out how he or she behaves in certain situations and what needs are likely underlying the behaviors.

These are questions that only you can answer about your child. There are no right or wrong answers, but they can help guide your understanding of what life is like for your child. Sure, some tasks and behaviors are typical for most kids at certain ages, but the exact timing and details of any one child's developmental road map are absolutely unique. At any given time, some kids move emotionally more quickly than others; other kids seem most focused on their physicality, as if ignoring cognitive or emotional dimensions of their experience. The very next month, these emphases could reverse 180 degrees! And no pattern is right or wrong.

- How comfortable is your child in her body? Does he seem timid or excited when facing a new physical activity?

- Does your child seem sensitive to changes in routine? What does she do if the routine is changed?
- Does your child express angry or sad feelings openly? How often does he or she have temper tantrums?
- How does your child show frustration? Does he shut down quietly and walk away in defeat? Does she throw herself on the floor, or stomp away mad?
- How often does your child enjoy solitary play?
- How often does your child enjoy playing side by side with other children he or she knows?
- How often is your child able to follow directions and listen to limits?
- Is your child always comfortable at good-byes? Does she tend to shut down, cry, or fall apart?
- How does your child behave in a new situation, such as visiting a friend's home or going to a birthday party? Does she take her time and observe first? Does he need to stay with you for a while? Does he run in and explore with interest from the start?

As you move through this book, you may come back to these questions and find you are responding differently. Why? Because how your child handles life and herself is always in flux. Keep these as a guide, a way to think of your changing, growing child over the span of years that are so dynamic!

chapter three

Toddler's-Eye View

Shift Your POV and Change Your Interaction with Your Child

Parenting from your child's point of view means shifting in orientation: instead of understanding your toddler from a "top-down" adult position, think and look at the world as if you were their age and their size. Thinking like a toddler means seeing many things as new, fascinating, or scary; it means having no real sense of time, and an unending curiosity about life. It means not knowing why things happen or what came before. From this vantage point, it makes sense that when toddlers have an idea, they act on it right away.

Clearly, the world looks different from this position. Adults usually think in a rational and logical progression, where events are sequenced in time. Young children do not. As one mother of a three-year-old reported:

For weeks, my son battled me every night at bedtime—he just would NOT go to sleep. He'd ask for "one more thing" over and over. He was always begging, "Stay with me. I miss you. DON'T GO!" I was yelling. I was shutting his door. I was pleading, "Pleeaase go to sleep." It could take us up to two hours and I was furious by the time he'd go to sleep. I clearly was not helping the situation. What turned it around was when I really got to see that bedtime meant "good-bye" to him, just like when I leave for work each day. What I saw as the end of the day, and my time for myself, he saw as yet another separation. After speaking to Tovah, I took a different approach. Just like I do every morning, I gave him a kiss on each cheek so he could have me with him through his sleep. I told him, "I will see you in the morning, just like I always do, but my kisses are with you all night." It took a few nights for the new routine and the reassurance to set in, and then the battles were gone.

Another parent turned around a common irritating behavior: his two-and-a-half-year-old daughter got great pleasure from throwing her toys and watching her father yell and scream and tell her "no." He tried time-outs; he tried taking away her toys. Both strategies failed and the father's frustration escalated.

Instead of fighting the girl's behavior, I encouraged him "to go with it," but in a reasonable and limited way. My suggestion? That he give her a place she *could* throw. Two-year-olds can be very impulsive. They are testing out their power ("oooh—I throw this and it goes far!") as well as the power they have with parents ("I throw this, and Daddy yells—how interesting").

The father was reluctant and said, "I don't want to encourage her to do it more."

I assured him that the opposite would happen.

From the child's view, throwing is fun and it gets a reaction from daddy. Joining her would both take away his overreaction and let her know that he understood her desire for throwing. Initially, he stayed with time-outs and removing toys. The behavior continued and increased. Feeling at his wits' end, he got a small trash can and played the throw-it-in-the-can game, telling her she could throw toys in anytime. Soon she tired of the game and was rarely throwing. Toddlers want to be understood and validated in their desires. That is what this father did by giving his daughter a designated place to throw. (Small basketball hoops, placed low, can work, too.)

How parents approach this shift in view varies. And it can take time. In the examples above, the mother had an "a-ha!" moment when I noted that bedtime was the biggest separation of the day, and the hardest one. Quickly she reframed bedtime like the morning separation and the child was more comforted and able to go to sleep without a fight.

Seeing the world from a toddler's view can be an odd experience. After all, we are socialized adults. The idea that we would suddenly lunge a cup of water across the room or shove a child out of our way just because he was there is simply bizarre. Eventually, when the father agreed to let the child throw toys in a specified place, the behavior passed because he finally understood that her urge to throw was big. Once she felt understood, the behavior passed.

The point is not to be too hard on yourself, and to keep in mind that these years of toddlerhood are part of a much longer process. It is an opportunity, however, to consider your own attitudes and expectations about how you think toddlers *should* behave. Sometimes we are not even aware of our own assumptions or biases that might be preventing us from thinking from a child's view, or from remembering that their point of view is decidedly different from our own.

Often parents' knee-jerk reaction in the face of a tyrannical two-year-old who wants to boss everyone around, or a seemingly manipulative four-year-old who refuses to take responsibility for any of his actions, is either to try to control them through strong discipline and rules or to give up control entirely. Confused, embarrassed, and upset by the "outrageous" behavior being shown in front of them, parents clamp down and try to eliminate the bothersome behaviors. The unspoken attitude or belief of the parent is "I need to nip this behavior in the bud before it gets any worse."

At the opposite extreme, some parents give up entirely, justifying a hands-in-the-air approach with all sorts of excuses: "She is so strong-willed, I don't want to smother that energy." "I just can't fight with him anymore—I think he'll outgrow it." Or, "Isn't this what toddlers are supposed to do?"

Most parents swing between the two extremes, asserting rules and order (top-down) or giving up. If there are two parents, they may split sides—one taking the "control the behavior/nip it in the bud" approach and the other throwing up their hands. And while there is no such thing as a perfect parent, and we have *all* gone to both these extremes—sometimes in a single afternoon—there is a more productive way for you to interact with your child, a way that will help ground your child in the safety and assurance he needs as he navigates separation and his striving for self.

You can and will find a kind of toddlertopia—that state of enjoying your toddlers, loving them, and embracing them, in all their ups and downs and paradoxical behaviors—without giving up your parental authority. In fact, you will feel even more equipped to parent your toddler. Parents say that once they make this shift, they feel calmer and more competent as a parent. Perhaps even more important, you will also be able to truly maximize this critical time in your child's life so that he or she can develop the resilience, determination, and brain skills for their future happiness and achievement.

The Five Steps to Parenting from Your Child's Point of View

The following five action steps will help you see the world through your toddler's eyes without giving up your authority. The parent is the one who provides the road map for their child. These five principles will help you shift your orientation and understand your child and your own reactions so that you can better attune to experience and what they need, and adapt your response accordingly.

1. Stay Close, Even When It's Hard

Our kids need us. They need us to stay close even when they are pushing us away. They need us to be (or at least act!) steady when they falter. They need us to stay calm even when they are agitated, upset, or plain difficult to manage. Why? Because we are their rock, the person they count on when the going gets tough. We are the biggest, most important constant in their lives, and they need repeated, concrete reminders that we love them, can take care of them, and will respond to most—if not all—of their needs, regardless of how they behave, respond, or feel. We are still there for them, no matter what they do or say, even when they misbehave. Does this mean giving in all the time? Certainly not. But it does mean learning to accept that our children are good sometimes and bad sometimes (you'll revisit this when they are teenagers!). Sometimes they make us proud, and sometimes we cannot believe how they act. But our children need to know that we still love them even when they have a hard time or do things we don't like, or when we set a limit or steer them in a different direction.

2. You're in Charge

How does this impact us? It's often hard to stay calm and carry on! We forget how little and vulnerable they actually are. Especially when our toddlers' behavior is confusing, irrational, and frustrating to us. Diane and Mark were parents of an only child. They described their daughter as a "dream child"—happy, easy to calm, slept well by six weeks, easy to distract, even as a young toddler. At two, she never had a tantrum, and they could take her anywhere. She would sit at the table, eat most anything, and rarely whined or cried. She even played on her own! People complimented them on what great parents they were to have such a terrific toddler. But then Leila approached three and, according to the mother, "became a different child overnight, like a switch went off," hard to handle, wouldn't listen, no longer agreeable, and when she was told "No," no matter how kindly or how firmly, she just did that thing more, or demanded louder.

Leila discovered a towel bar she could just reach in the kitchen. She'd reach up high and grasp it. Her mother would tell her, "Don't pull on that," worrying it would break, and Leila would back off. But over time, when her mother said this, Leila would look at her, not let go, and laugh. Or she would let go but immediately reach for it again. From Leila's view, the interaction was now a game. The mother continued in her kind, gentle tone to try to reason with her: "Leila, sweetie, you know I have told you that will break and I don't want you to get hurt."

The mother was being kind and reasonable (although underneath she was getting increasingly frustrated). But Leila would have none of it. Leila was on another track. She was discovering her power. How far can I push mommy? Does she really mean that I have to stop? Oh, look, mommy keeps saying not to do it—over and over. Leila looked at her and held on even tighter. Now Leila lifted her legs so that she was dangling from it. Her mother feared the bar would break from the wall. She went over and kindly asked her to stop, explaining that this was not safe. Leila laughed and laughed until her mother physically and firmly removed her from the bar, stating clearly that Leila could not do this, it was unsafe. Leila did not try it again, as a clear limit had been set. But then the mother felt guilty—"Should I have pried her hands off of the bar, like I did? Was that too intrusive? Was I wrong?"

Sometimes parents get confused this way. Toddlers need limits and they look to us to be the authority and let them know when to stop. Not in rigid ways, but in ways that keep them safe. In the example above, the mother is being a rational adult. Leila is living in a place where she tests out her power with excitement and glee. But she also counts on her mother to distinctly tell her when a limit is needed. Instead, the mother used the same gentle tone she always does, rather than being clear that this was unsafe and could not continue. Sometimes parents forget that they are authority. I asked Diane why she had not firmly told Leila that this was not okay, had taken her away from it and moved on. The mother was hesitant and then said, "I thought I had to be kind and gentle and supportive all the time. I never want to raise my voice. I don't want to upset her. I want her to always count on me."

I have heard this interpretation from other parents. Some parents are afraid of having their children get upset with them, and try to keep it from happening (and yes, children do get upset when they are told "no" or a limit is set!). Handling it this way prevents the child from knowing what the limit is; in fact, children cannot learn to handle being upset if they are not allowed to even get upset. By allowing children their upset and anger, they learn (over time) to handle these emotions. Just as important, they learn that even if they get upset with mommy or daddy, they will still be taken care of. It may seem ironic, but setting limits actually builds children's trust. They know they can count on us.

3. Be Consistent (Mostly)

Consistency helps ground toddlers. Consistency makes it easier for parents to manage their children's fluctuations. But what does consistency mean? What does it look like? Being consistent doesn't require rigidity. Think of consistency as a framework for the child's day. A frame of "usually, we do things this way." But not always, and even within daily routines, details can vary. If, most of the time, children are organized by routines, are made to feel safe, secure, and loved, then they are much more likely to roll with the punches when routines are broken. Why? Because they had routines and consistency as their daily base, and they trust that it will return again. Routines are their "home base." Similar to the secure base that helps them feel safe enough to go out and explore, routines organize their days, giving them the grounding needed to handle change. Kids are indeed resilient if you let them be!

Being consistent means first establishing routines. (More on that in chapter 5.) Everyone talks about routines for young children. Why? They are a bedrock for toddlers who lack any sense of time. Even at five, their sense of time (although better than at two) is still vague. After all, time is abstract. You can't see it. You can't touch it. It is a "sense" that increases as children develop. For adults, it is hard to imagine not setting up our days around a time sequence, or not knowing what fifteen minutes really means or feels like. Toddlers rely on us to set up the organization of their day, to cue them into what is next, to help them get through one activity (for example, breakfast) and guide them to the next (for example, *now we are getting shoes on to leave the house*).

Because toddlers lack this sense of time, and their brains are still developing, they have not internalized the skills that adults (well most, anyway) use to help them manage time, control their impulses, express their needs, thoughtfully plan their actions, and cope with stress. These are the executive functions or "life skills" I discussed in the second chapter. We as parents begin to help them build these skills during the toddler years so that as they get older—school-aged and beyond—they have the ability to do this more for themselves. Research verifies the importance of these executive functions for success in many areas of life. It is the consistency and repeated routines at this age that are a crucial part of laying the foundation children need to thrive when managing the complexity later in life. Daily repeated routines make life more predictable and give toddlers an inner feeling of security. They know that books come after bath; that after the Curious George TV show is over, we get shoes to go outside. That feels good to know. Otherwise every new activity is a surprise (or shock!). Toddlers thrive on routines!

Even though young children lack these skills, they absolutely need to feel organized. In truth, toddlers are not alone. Most people—children, adults, teens—don't do well if they feel disorganized; it is an unsettling feeling. A major role for parents and caregivers is to help organize their toddler, as a way to help them eventually do it for themselves. What do I mean by organization? An internalized feeling that there is a rhythm to the day, a framework for the order of things and how the day flows. When there is a feeling of being organized internally, the child feels safe and secure, making them better able to enjoy life and manage the ups and downs of their day. Without that feeling of organization, they fall apart (adults do, too!). The opposite of organization is disorganization or chaos. That is not a feeling anyone likes, and especially not young children.

Establish routines to structure the life of your toddler—for meals, for getting dressed, for bedtime and bathtime, for getting out the door. Routines give the child cues and a sense of "what happens now? And what happens next?" For example: "I hear the bathwater running, now I take a bath. After bath, I'll get my pj's on, and then we read a book." Routines are not about rigid rules. I think of them more as little orange flags that guide the child throughout the day, a child who might otherwise careen off the track: "time for breakfast," "time for lunch," "time for school," "this is the way we eat at the table," "this is the way we take a bath safely."

This is not to say that you have to treat every day, every routine with rigidity. Kids can be—and should be—enormously resilient if a routine is broken or altered on occasion. In fact, each time a routine changes (for example, grandparents visit for the weekend) and you later return to the regular routine, the child is learning how to be flexible. This is especially true when you recognize and label the disruption: "This weekend, we didn't eat lunch in the kitchen like we usually do because Grandma and Grandpa were visiting. But now we are back in our same seats at the kitchen table." Routines also have to be flexible since toddlers' needs change. When your younger toddler moved from two naps to one, she adjusted. The day changed a bit, but the basic routine continued, just with one nap less.

4. Be Realistic

In order for our children to emerge on the other side of separation feeling confident, resilient, and self-assured, we as parents need to have realistic expectations of what our children can and can't do. Yes, all kids are different, in style and expression of these qualities. But they are similar in this fundamental way: they need to know you are there for them no matter what they do. And showing them they can count on you, so they can summon the courage to become who they are meant to be, means being reasonable in what you expect of them.

One afternoon, a four-and-a-half-year-old and her two-year-old sister were left unsupervised for a few minutes when their grandmother answered the door. The younger sister took the opportunity to put a whole roll of toilet paper into the toilet. When her older sister ran and got her grandmother, the grandmother laughed and shook her head, smiling at the younger sister.

Later that day, the four-and-a-half-year-old called grandma over and when she arrived, she was holding a roll of toilet paper up in the bathroom, as if she, too, would put it in. But this time, the grandmother got angry and scolded the older sister, who broke down in tears. Why had grandma laughed at the two-year-old sister?

Some parents see this kind of behavior at this age as manipulative. But there may be another way to look at it. The older girl was jealous, and felt that if she acted like her babyish sister, she, too, could get positive attention. When the need for attention is addressed and a limit is put up in a reasonable way, meaning, "You don't have to do that, I can give you attention," the situation can shift and her need will be met.

In other words, the response to the four-year-old has to be

quite different from the response to the two-year-old. Age is one context for understanding what is reasonable.

It is easy to lose hold of what is realistic to expect of a child. Think of when you see moments or even days and weeks of progression—the two-year-old not asking for his pacifier, the three-year-old taking the initiative to put on her socks before her shoes just as you've been coaching her, or the four-year-old finally being able to leave the house without protest or delay—these same kids may not always be up to the task each and every day (or may not even do it twice in a day!). Again, this is a time of great fluctuation. If that "obedient" two-year-old is off his schedule, or some other change has impacted his life (he gets a cold or his babysitter goes away on vacation), he just may regress and act out screaming his head off for his "binky." Your proud three-year-old may one morning look at her socks and shoes and throw them across the room instead of putting them on to show she's ready to leave for school.

It's times like these when you need to be realistic and keep in mind that Teddy is still only two years old. He does not always remember to tell you when he has to go to the bathroom. He does not recall feeling safe and secure yesterday without his pacifier. Four-year-old Kerry might have shown you that she's "a big girl" by sleeping in her "big girl bed" for four nights straight. But when the weekend comes, and the new routine is broken, it should not be surprising that she becomes hysterical as she faces her room alone with only a night-light for comfort. And your four-year-old who left the house on Friday with total ease? On Monday, after a weekend together with his family, he can't find his backpack, and he'll collapse on the floor because the wrong coat is on the hook.

These regressions are normal. Every time your child takes a step forward toward growing up more (whether that is using the toilet, sleeping in a bed, starting school, or mastering the jungle gym at the playground), they also are reminded of how much they need you. They don't like to feel on their own completely (even if they act as if they do!). That would be too scary. As one five-year-old said the same week he learned to ride a two-wheeler bike: "I won't ever go to college, or get married, or get too big. I just want to be with you, Mommy, forever." A three-and-a-half-year-old, newly in a big bed, requested: "When I grow up, can we get a bigger house and I can live in it with you and my new bed?" These examples show that the feeling of achieving something "big" is both exhilarating (*I did it! I have freedom! I am big!*) and terrifying.

It is also confusing for parents. One mother noted that her nearly three-year-old mastered using the toilet and was done with diapers within a week of starting. The mother was happily surprised. But then she noted that her daughter was using lots of baby talk again and sucking her thumb more. This example reminds us they are so big and yet so little, all at once. In chapter 7, I say more about how to handle this part of growing up and the toddler's need to be babied so they are able to grow up.

We need to be realistic about exactly where our children are developmentally and what other things are going on that might trigger setbacks in behavior. Development moves in fits and starts, rather than a clear and straight pathway. What is good one day is not the next. As one mother noted of her two-and-a-half-year-old, "I finally got her to stop throwing food at mealtime, and we had our first relaxing dinner. But then, two days later she climbed out of the crib and now won't go to sleep. If I had my choice, I'd go back to a little food throwing!" The key is to resist getting swept up in their orbit so that we feel out of control (and forget that we are the adults), which makes our kids feel even less in control.

By giving your child clear guidelines that align with realistic expectations, and keeping a good sense of humor, you pave the way for them to eventually learn they indeed can calm down, can follow directions, can sleep on their own. Realistic expectations include knowing that when development moves forward, and you think you are beyond some hurdle of challenging behavior, you just might be. But in some other area, your child may take a few steps back and regress.

Even minor disruptions can impact the toddler. It's not always easy for parents to keep in mind that some changes in a schedule can upset the applecart, or that the situation the child is in may not be ideal for her. For instance, is it realistic for the two-year-old to "be nice" at a family party if she has skipped her nap two days in a row, or even if she has napped but there is a room full of people? Is it reasonable to expect that a three-year-old is going to behave in a toy store? Or for a four-year-old to sit quietly through an hour-long show? As parents, we don't always recognize that change has even occurred or that a situation may not be right for a child's age. A parent being away for a business meeting, even if they go often, is still a change for a toddler. Grandparents visiting, no matter how much fun, is a change. An hour-long concert, even if it is child-friendly, is still a long time. Just going from weekend to Monday feels like a big change to children two to five. And we can expect regression or meltdowns when change is part of their lives.

5. Make the Boundaries Clear

Maintaining our boundaries with our own children helps us to stay objective so that we are not swept up into toddler orbit, that haze of half-formed thoughts and intense feelings, of muddling around in a three-year-old landscape. Or the anger and frustration of a four-year-old who feels nothing is "fair" to him. Being clear about our own baggage helps. But sometimes parents find that they have personality or temperament differences with their child that seem to be exacerbating the push-pull dynamic so characteristic of how toddlers interact with their parents or caregivers.

Just as small children are not mini adults, our children are also not exactly "like us." Indeed, many parents are confused and frustrated when they rub up against a child who is different in temperament and personality. This is especially true when our child has a characteristic or style that we do not understand, are frustrated by, or simply find unappealing. Sometimes it is an attribute different from who we are. Other times it is a quality in the child that we also embody, an insecurity or other behavior we don't like in ourselves.

One mother prided herself on how social she was and how deeply rooted her friendships were. "Nothing matters more in life than having close friends you can count on." She could not understand why friendship was not important to her five-year-old. "I just don't get him. He is happy to be with his sister. Other kids like him but he doesn't seem to care. He never gets called on playdates, he doesn't ask to play with any one child. Seems like any child is fine for him, but he doesn't have one close friend." In this case, the parents were athletic and recalled how much both of them loved being part of sports teams. Their child, in contrast, was small in stature, and artistic and musical. A mismatch? For sure. But stepping back and recognizing that he is not the same person they are will allow them to be better parents.

In another example, a father was upset by his gentle and kindhearted three-year-old, who shied away from physically active and aggressive kids, and backed off from any kind of rough play. The father recalled being left out by other children—he had been small for his age, and often found himself afraid. Seeing his child with similar qualities infuriated him and kept him from supporting his child in positive ways.

A mother had expressed concern about her two-and-a-half-year-old's lack of ability to interact with other toddlers. Even my assurance that he was still young did not help, so I suggested we watch him together when he was at the center. This little boy was standing to the side of the room, watching other children play, looking quite interested in what they were doing, but keeping a distance that felt safe to him. It looked to me like he was observing, taking things in, and thinking about what was going on, but it felt different to this mother. "Do you see how afraid he is? He is scared, afraid no one will like him," she commented. I asked what made her think that; after all, he was not even three years old. "I know the feeling," she said. "The kids never wanted to play with me. It is a terrible feeling."

We need to distinguish between our own past and what is really about our children in order to see our children for who they are (not for who we wish them to be).

• What You Bring to the Table •

Where do you fit in? That's a tough question. We all bring our own histories (read: baggage) with us when we become parents. It's important to become aware of who you are in relation to your child, and how your own attitudes, expectations, and experiences may be shadowing your parenting approach. You may come to realize some surprising ways that your own experience is getting played out in your relationship with your own child!

Being aware of what biases we bring from our own upbringing and life experiences is not easy. But I can promise you this much: when we have more objectivity and see ourselves as separate from our children and their behavior, we are much more likely to be able to guide our children in a loving, supportive, yet firm way. And we become better parents. Establishing this first boundary is about you getting to know yourself, identifying your triggers (what behaviors or roles set you off? Are there things your child does that really get to you? Make you mad or frustrated?) and knowing your personality (how you relate, what situations are easy or hard for you). The better you know yourself and can reflect on how you relate and react, the more you will be able to step back and see who your child is, separate from you. It's also about thinking back on how you were raised and what you bring into your relationship with your child. When your child has a behavior that is driving you nuts (what that is varies for every parent), it helps to think about why. If you can't stand her talking back to you, as when she says, "I don't have to do that!" think about what that triggers for you. Were you never allowed to defy your parents? Were your parents overly strict and you always followed the rules, even if you felt misunderstood?

Parents often get caught up in their own experience when they observe their toddlers showing "rude" behavior. Your child won't say hello to grandma, or hides rather than greets someone. This can feel shaming to you if you were always expected to say please and thank you, greet with eye contact, and be polite. You may think, *What a rude child I have. I could never have done that!* In fact, however, this could be age-appropriate and your child needs your support to move beyond this stage. In other words, the better you know yourself and your own upbringing, the more you will be able to understand your responses to your child. And that helps maintain the boundary for a parent to see just what their child needs.

When we understand our own biases about how children should behave (and where these biases come from), how we should act as parents, and what the "appropriate" dynamic is to use, then it's much easier to figure out what might be complicating our present situation with our own toddlers.

When a toddler turns into a demanding "benign dictator," which can happen around age two and a half or three, some parents get pulled into the toddler's orbit. Rather than seeing it for what it is—the child's need to test power—parents can become part of the control battle. One mother was knocked off her loving parenting course at this point in her daughter's development. Her sweet baby turned into a bossy and stubborn three-year-old. This mother was battling with her as if she were much older, over what clothes to wear, what food she would eat, how many toys she could take when they left the house, what coat to put on. It was battle after battle. When the mother spoke about this, she sounded like she was describing a teenager. Had I not known the child, I would have thought she was a sixteen-year-old. The mother denied that the child reminded her of anyone she knew, now or in her past. I was puzzled as to why she could not see that the child was three. But after several parenting sessions the mother revealed that she had a highly demanding and bossy older sister who to this day continued to scrutinize and criticize her. As much as the mother had looked up to her sister, she felt she could never satisfy her. She was still trying to win her approval. This relationship was blocking the mother from seeing the needs of her child at three. Instead, it felt like she was battling with her impossible to please sister. Once she became aware of this, she pulled back. She did not take her child so personally. In fact, she started to admire the girl's strength, which was something the mother lacked in the face of her sister, and found the behaviors funny. She stopped battling her. Quickly, the child's need for control subsided. This is one example of the past blocking a parent's ability to see what a child needs.

Here's another example: Trina came from a family that had few rules. She reported that her parents "let me do whatever I wanted." They were not very involved in her day-to-day life, but she felt they listened to her. "When I did not want to do something, they said fine, they never battled it." Since she had graduated from a top-tier college and had a successful career as well as raising her three children, she felt that not ever forcing her children (ages two, four, and eight) to do things when they said no was fine. In contrast, her husband came from a family that had strict rules and high standards at all times: "Never give up. Start something and you finish it. No exceptions." He chalked his own success up to this must-do attitude. Not surprisingly, the couple often disagreed about how to approach parenting. It came to a head one day on the street. They left their house to go to a friend's, just three blocks away. Their four-year-old complained that it was too far to walk and he was too tired. He sat down on the sidewalk, pouted, and would not budge. The father sternly insisted he get up and walk. The mother tried to cajole and joke with him. Nothing worked. Finally, Trina decided they would drive the three blocks. The father was furious. *Who was right?* they asked me. I was less concerned about the right way to handle this one situation than the ongoing battle they had. The father's past made it hard for him to see that sometimes going with what their child wanted was okay, even if that meant not doing what the parents asked. And the mother's past made it hard for her to ever set a firm limit or say no. Both were responding to their pasts rather than seeing the child's needs in the present.

Parents who have trouble accepting their own negative thoughts, feelings, or behaviors tend to have more trouble dealing with their children's demonstrations of anger, defiance, or "badness." After all, it is not easy to reconcile and accept the parts of ourselves we don't like! Some parents will take it personally when the child misbehaves or says negative things like "I hate you!" This can be especially true for parents who never rebelled or defied their own parents as children. They "sucked it up" and were always good and so had to harbor their own negative feelings and never express them. Some parents are still trying to win their own parents' approval, and never disagree with them, even as an adult. In this case, it can be hard to face your own children's negative emotions and behaviors in ways that support what they need at this age. Accepting that we, as adults, have good and bad parts of ourselves, including qualities we don't like or are ashamed of, helps us take a step back and see our children for who they are.

Parenting POV
What We Bring from Our Past

I've assembled a set of questions to help you identify characteristics that may unwittingly be affecting your interactions with your child. You may be surprised at how the way you were raised is impacting your attitude toward parenting!

Think about the questions and your responses; you may even want to write down your response in a notebook or journal. The intention is to help you get a better sense of your past and what you bring to parenting your own children. When we as parents are aware of how our own childhoods shape who we are and how we respond to our children (in ways good or bad), we can better understand what our children need and then shift our responses to best support them. Think about the following questions from your childhood in terms of how you were raised and what your school and peer experiences were like. Use these reflections to better understand yourself as a parent today and the ways you respond to your child.

Home and Family

Think about growing up in your family:

1. What was your general family feeling? Warm, caring, and loving? Parents who accepted you for who you were, the good and the bad? Were your parents more distant and cold, even if loving? A family riddled with conflicts, tension, or breakups?
2. Were your parents strict, with clear rules to follow? Were you punished or shamed if you did not follow their rules? Did you have to "toe a line" with your parents and behave in acceptable ways, no matter how you felt?
3. Were your opinions listened to, respected, and taken into consideration?
4. Were saying "please" and "thank you" and being well-mannered required of you?
5. Were you allowed to show anger openly if you were upset with your parents? Did you keep anger inside and quietly seethe and not let them know? Did you ever talk back to your parents or openly disagree with them?

6. If you have siblings: Were you close to them, even if it was love-hate (fighting one moment, playing the next)? How do you relate now?
7. Did you feel overshadowed by one—a sibling who was a "superstar" or "golden child"? One who struggled in life, needed excessive attention, or you were responsible for? Did you feel you had to make up for what they could not do?
8. Were you bossed around by an older sibling or always trying to win their approval?
9. Were your parents critical of your actions, decisions, or behavior? Did they question your choices or judgment? Did they respect your ideas, choices, and decisions, even if they were different from theirs?
10. If you felt overwhelmed by life or upset, were your parents there for you—caring and supportive? What about when you messed up or made mistakes?
11. Were you ashamed to face your parents if you made mistakes, little or big ones?
12. Did you ever feel terribly ashamed about something you'd done, worried about telling your parents—and their reaction was kind and accepting?
13. Did your parents give loving support regardless of what you did? Was their love based more on your accomplishments or on you doing something that made them happy?
14. How did you feel when you let your parents down? Did you feel they would forgive you and understand? Did you worry you'd lose their love and approval?
15. Did you work hard to seek your parents' approval? Do you feel you got it?

School

Think about your time at school as a child:

1. What are your memories? Was school a place you enjoyed being? Something you had to endure, neither good nor bad? Something you worried about, disliked, or dreaded?
2. How did you do in school? Did you do well? Were you an all-around top student? Did you listen and follow the rules? Maybe even a teacher's pet?
    - Did you excel in some areas but struggle in others?
    - Did you feel smart? Proud? Ashamed? Dumb?
    - Did you feel you were not smart, even if you did well?
    - Worried people would discover you were not as smart as they thought you were?
3. Were school and learning hard for you?
    - Were you a class clown or troublemaker? Did you challenge authority?
    - Were you ever asked to leave a school, suspended, or thrown out?
    - Did you find it hard to sit or focus? Or did you feel bored and uninterested?
4. Did your parents show you they were proud of your school success? Criticize your progress, no matter how well you did? Not pay much attention? Always expect you to excel more, no matter how well you did? Not expect much from you academically?
5. Did you feel that not doing well (in school, sports, or another activity) would be hurtful to your parents? That it would let them down somehow?

6. Did you excel in one area at a very high level, such as a sport, music, art, or a specific academic endeavor? Did it take immense training, practice, and focus to excel? Do you believe that your child needs to learn discipline, hard work, and perseverance from a very young age in order to succeed?

Peers and Social Experience

Think about your experiences with peers and friendships growing up:

1. What were your experiences like with other children? Were you generally comfortable in the social arena, or more like an outsider or disliked kid? A social butterfly with many friends?
2. Did you prefer to socialize in groups of children, or just one or two friends at a time?
3. Do you have memories of a best friend, or close, caring friendships and good times with peers?
4. Were you left out by other children, bossed around, or picked on? Were kids mean to you? Do you remember a bully, or someone you feared, even if they left you alone?
5. Do you recall longing to play with another child but not feeling welcomed or not knowing how to make friends?

These questions are meant to help you reflect on what you bring into your own parenting today. Take some time to think about how your experience as a child is similar to or different from the relationship you are creating with your own child.

• Good Enough Parenting •

Establishing the safe boundaries and limits children need at this time in their lives does not require controlling your children. It does not mean using the force of your will or your voice to discipline your child into submission. But it also doesn't mean giving up and letting your child rule the roost. Try instead learning to understand toddlers from *their* point of view by remembering that you are the adult in charge. This can be a profound shift in the way we usually parent. When parents understand why toddlers behave the way they do, when they have a clearer understanding of the main developmental challenges that *all* toddlers are trying to meet, then suddenly parents can guide their child instead of control them.

What does it mean to show our love and acceptance, even when our toddler is acting in ways we don't like, don't understand, or that drive a parent crazy? That's the challenge of good-enough parenting during the toddler years. Even in our toddler program, with two- and three-year-olds, the children need the reassurance they are still accepted, especially if they feel they have done something wrong. Three-year-old Charlie had just learned his mother was going to have a baby. This was exciting and worrisome news for him. What did it mean? Wasn't he her baby? He came to school excited and wound-up. At the Play-Doh table he wanted all the red Play-Doh for himself and made sure to scoop up as much as he could. When another child came over to join him, he immediately stuck his arm out, pushed him away, and quickly grabbed on to his Play-Doh. "No! *I* have all the Play-Doh!" The teacher recognized his need to be alone and keep the Play-Doh. She validated this need: "We always have enough Play-Doh for you. But I can't let you hurt anyone."

He immediately got quiet and looked away. This is the moment that the toddler doubts he is loved anymore. It might sound extreme, but it is true. The teacher reached over to him to give reassurance, saying, "I still love you, even when you grab all the Play-Doh." Feeling reassured (and relieved), he quickly perked up and pounded the dough.

When our toddlers are so fluctuating and erratic, it can be very stressful on us as parents. We want to pull our hair out, we lose our tempers, we wonder what we are doing wrong, we can regress, and we can even fall back on unproductive ways of interacting with our kids. We've all been there. There is no such thing as a perfect parent. A mother of a four-year-old noted that "I knew I had to change how I parented when my son said so sweetly to me, 'Mommy, today you were good—you did not yell at me. You get a sticker.'" And as another parent said, "My daughter started yelling at me to go to time-outs when I screamed at her. I knew something had to change."

Change is a must. Self-awareness is, too.

chapter four

Toddler Shame

What Happens When You Don't *Think Like a Toddler*

When we inadvertently (or even at times purposefully) try to control our children or resist understanding the world from their point of view, we not only set up a negative parent/child relationship; we also undermine the very person our child is trying to become. A child's sense of self is very much still a work-in-progress that can easily be thrown off a positive course. The idea of self (who am I?) is not yet stable or fully formed. Just as the brain is in a rapidly moving stage of development, far from being completely formed, the same is true for that internal sense of identity, confidence, and assurance, pieces central to long-term achievement and success. This is why toddlers are so vulnerable to the way in which we interact with them. And as we are the main model in their lives, the one they trust and rely on, our parental responses matter. A lot. So what happens when we try to control them, or keep approaching their behaviors from an adult point of view? The pitfall is that we unwittingly cause them shame.

Shame is a feeling directed at the core sense of self. When the self is still new and being formed, when the toddler is forward looking and moving full speed ahead, shame can cut through and cause a lot of unnecessary pain. Indeed, shame can stunt the growth of a child. When we cajole them into bed, pressure them to get out the door in the morning, push them to eat particular foods, wear certain outfits, and be nice and share, we are trying to manage their behavior in a well-intentioned but misguided attempt to teach our children about life and relationships, or merely keep them safe, all of which can backfire. In today's busy and pressurized parenting climate, there's very little of their lives that we don't try to manage—all at an age when a child's every instinct says "I have to do this myself!" But for toddlers, who are just starting to develop their independence, the unintended consequence of parental control, or of failing to see their perspective, is that we cause them to feel they are bad, not good enough, or not valued. We shame them, even if we don't mean to.

• How Shame Blocks Empathy •

So why is shame so harmful at the toddler stage of development? Children this age are learning that sometimes they feel and do good things (happy, enjoyment, getting along with others) and sometimes they feel and do bad things (anger, fear, aggression, not listening). These are all natural feelings and responses at these ages and children need our help learning to accept that both good and bad reside within them. In fact, it is a struggle for some people long past this age, to accept that sometimes they are good and sometimes they are bad. But we need to work that out in order to become people who can admit when we do wrong without being so ashamed that we can't move on or apologize or fix our mistakes.

Accepting the bad parts of self is what shame works against. Children know how to be happy and feel good about themselves, but accepting the bad parts of self and negative feelings is much harder and can turn into a lifelong struggle. Shame can inhibit a child's ability to express his or her emotions freely and honestly right at this critical stage of brain and self development. Becoming so focused on and worried about being good or bad, can get in the way of their development. Instead of being curious and exploring and figuring out the world, they become focused on "Am I good? Am I good enough?" because they are afraid of making mistakes or being bad. When they are shamed by our parental responses into feeling "not good enough," the child can only go one of two ways: either they cut off their emotions so they cannot feel them, an "emotional paralysis," or they become enraged.

These extremes block out a child's natural connection to how he really feels—about himself, about his thoughts, about his needs and desires, and eventually about others. For this reason, shame gets in the way of the development of empathy. If a child is repeatedly made to feel ashamed, then he becomes preoccupied with himself and getting his needs met and an overwhelming belief that there is something wrong with him. He can't even begin to take on the task of relating to others, let alone caring for them.

Brain science is too new to identify the exact mechanism by which shame impedes healthy toddler development, but there is clear evidence of possible pathways for its harmful and lasting effects. Just as toxic stress early in life can interrupt a baby's brain development, situations of intense, relentless shaming likely interrupt a young child's ability to self-regulate. If a child is unable to read or understand her emotions openly, and if she is made to feel badly for having negative thoughts, behaviors, or emotions, how would she begin to manage these hard emotions? In being pushed to extremes by feelings of shame—either needing to shut down completely and withdraw inwardly or to become rageful—how could a child be expected to learn how to self-soothe and cope? Calm himself down enough to listen to teachers and follow directions? Feel that she will be okay even when things go wrong? Stay centered enough when stressed that he doesn't fly into a tantrum at the least provocation? Self-regulation, beginning in toddlerhood and carried forward as the child grows, is based on the idea that parents help a child when they are distressed and that the child learns that sometimes things don't feel good or don't go their way. Their parent is still available for them, no matter what. Shame runs completely counter to this steady parental presence. No wonder it can potentially interfere with healthy brain development.

Shame Interrupts Development

Of course, we don't plan to shame our children. We think we are helping them, doing our job as attentive parents. But that's the crux of the problem: *parenting is rarely what it seems to be.* As children are muddling through these first attempts to separate from you, in order to learn how to feed themselves, play by themselves, learn alone and in a group, socialize with others, address their bodily functions, sleep independently and restfully, manage emotions and frustration, process disappointments, tragedy, and other of life's curveballs—we need to avoid shaming them.

• How We Shame Our Children •

When parents use shame as a so-called management tool, unwittingly or not, they threaten their child's healthy development, because shame works against the child's naturally emerging self. It works against a child's ability to grow a core sense of who he or she is and instead instills a growing sense of self-doubt. You may be wondering why any parent would shame a child, someone they love. It's because most parents don't realize what they are doing. They don't understand that the way they speak to their children, embarrass their children, or try to control their children's behavior can cause shame. By trying too hard to direct their children's behavior "for their own good," they undermine their child's tender sense of self which, in turn, jeopardizes the development of the critical lifelong skills.

Think for a moment: Have you ever commented upon or criticized your child's choice of clothing? Spoken about him in front of other parents as if he were not there? We all have. As parents, we shame our children out of love, concern, and,

We've All Felt It

Shame. Just the word conjures deep memories of feeling your own head warm and heavy with worry and discomfort—in a classroom, at a friend's house. Did you make a mistake? Did you act foolishly? Did other children see? One strong word, a criticism, a laugh, or a rolling of the eyes and your lower lids filled with hot tears. What is your memory of shame? We all have one. And these memories are usually set down when we are very, very young, beginning as toddlers.

yes, power. By trying to assert who we think that child should be and how we think he should fit in the world, we inadvertently make our young children feel ashamed when they are at their most vulnerable. Obviously, we don't do this to harm our children; we are simply trying to protect our children and raise them with the best intentions and in the best way we know how. But that's exactly the problem: when we come to our children with a plan or a preconceived notion of who we want them to be, just as they are beginning to emerge into their own person, we unintentionally get in their way and interfere with their development. They do not know that we have preconceived notions of who we want them to be. All they know is that they are trying to become their own person. By asking them to behave in a specific way or be different from who they are just now, we deny who they are or what they are feeling. We make them feel ashamed for who they are, the needs they have, and the very sense of self that is delicately emerging.

Toddlers are notoriously headstrong and not very good listeners. They also tend to be extreme—either overly cautious and inhibited or not cautious at all. Indeed, this age group seems to be in perpetual motion. They are heedless explorers ready to take on the world without all the necessary skills yet in place. And that's the way we want them to be—curious and adventurous! It is from this place that self-confidence and the ability to take initiative emerge. The challenge for us as parents is in giving children between ages two and five enough freedom to start making some of their own choices, so they can start making—and owning—their mistakes. What we see as mistakes, they take as part of the natural process of growing.

Sound difficult? It may be for you, but it's not for them. Young children are not yet self-conscious or judgmental about their actions. They leap into activities and toward situations without thinking them through. They live in the moment. Jumping off the slide at full tilt? Building a beautiful sand castle just to destroy it? Wearing rain boots when it's sunny outside? These may seem like illogical choices to us, but they make perfect sense to a toddler. *New boots? Who cares if it is hot and sunny outside—these are my new boots!* Indeed, many of these choices make us parents very nervous. Our response? We tend to overcorrect and attempt to control them, which just makes them feel bad about themselves, which then results in shame.

So how do parents avoid pushing the shame button? They need to pull back and remember that their child is learning; learning means trial and error and figuring it out. For parents, this means backing off, directing less, withholding criticism, letting children try on their own, and refraining from correcting tasks we think are done incorrectly or from doing tasks for them. But it also means being there to help and comfort them when frustration, discomfort, and upset set in.

Take Jeremy, a three-year-old who had a penchant for one blue shirt. He insisted on wearing the same blue T-shirt to school—no matter the weather, no matter how dirty the shirt had become. Every day he and his mother would battle. His mother would chastise him, saying, "You can't wear that every day. It's not okay to wear the same clothes every day."

Jeremy would look at her blankly and stubbornly and say, "No, I need my blue shirt."

"You don't *need* your blue shirt. You can wear this red one or this blue one with the white stripes. It's still blue." His mother would try to cajole him.

"No."

Some days, Jeremy won the battle, and his mother would let him wear his favorite blue T-shirt. Other days, his mother would hide the blue T-shirt and Jeremy, in tears or dejected silence, would sulk off to school.

What's going on here? Let's look at the situation from both

Jeremy's and his mom's points of view. First, when Jeremy says he needs his blue shirt, he means that sincerely. He *needs* it for comfort, for security, for love. At some point, this T-shirt began to gather meaning for him. There is comfort in keeping things the same, and at this young age, his knowing what he needs is a very big deal. We want our young children to know what they need and understand what comforts them. This helps them feel good about themselves; this makes them feel safe deep down—an ability and a feeling that will carry them forward through their entire lives.

Jeremy's mom, however, is thinking like her adult self: *Jeremy should not wear the same clothes to school every day. He needs to learn to act his age. I don't want him to feel embarrassed.*

Unfortunately, Jeremy doesn't have the ability to understand that his mother means well. All Jeremy takes from this ongoing battle is that his choice and need for his blue T-shirt are wrong. By telling him he doesn't need his blue shirt, his mother unintentionally has made Jeremy feel bad for wanting the shirt for comfort. But since he knows how much he needs it, he'll continue to battle for it.

These kinds of remarks by a parent cannot be filtered by young children; all they hear is "I'm not okay as I am" or "There is something wrong with me" or "Mommy doesn't like me." Of course, none of this is true, but young children don't have the intellectual or emotional capacity to understand where their parents are coming from. Nor should they. Young children live in a world that starts (and ends) with what they need. So the well-intentioned parent corrections get simplified to *I must be bad for needing what I need.*

Another example: Your three-year-old is transfixed by building blocks. He lines them up and then messes up the line. He piles up the blocks, carefully and with focus, and then all of a sudden he knocks them down. You often find yourself saying, "Honey, that's not the way you do it. You should try this—make a building. Don't knock them down. That's messy." You show him how to make a lovely tower.

Here's another very common situation. Your almost three-year-old loves puzzles. You are so excited because you know puzzles are a great learning tool. When you sit down on the floor with the pieces spread out, you notice that your daughter is becoming frustrated as she attempts to fit certain pieces into slots where they don't fit. Worried about her getting too frustrated, you jump in and show her: "Here, Ally, this is how you do it!" After all, she should be happy you showed her how to complete it. Maybe next time she will copy you and do it herself.

Instead of being happy at the puzzle piece fitting, Ally pushes away the puzzle and stomps off.

You are left confused and a little upset.

"Come back, come back. Let's try it again!" You worry that she doesn't see tasks through to the end and wonder if she'll ever persist at something hard.

What just happened?

When you stepped in to "fix" the situation by putting the puzzle piece in the correct place, you inadvertently sent your daughter the message that she couldn't do it. Yes, she was frustrated at not being able to figure it out. But by interfering, rather than helping her manage the frustration (see chapter 6 for more on this topic), you took away the opportunity for her to wrestle through the situation, make a mistake, and *want* to try again, whether now or another time. This type of well-intentioned behavior takes away the child's initiative, or desire to try, try again, another time. The takeaway message for Ally? *Making a mistake is bad; I did it wrong. Mommy doesn't think I can do it on my own. I can't do it.*

These are everyday situations, none of which is too serious on its own. But when parents or caregivers regularly overcorrect an error, chastise a choice, or are too quick to fix something, a child feels shame in a way that interferes with his growing sense of self and attitude toward his own learning.

Of course, it's very natural for parents to correct their child. You know you can show your child how best to do something—from choosing an outfit to completing a shape sorter game. But it's your child who is in the place of learning. Sometimes as adults we assume that learning is a simple and linear process that follows a pattern of "I show you so you can know how to do it." Unfortunately, that is not how learning works. It is a process that unfolds alongside the child's budding discovery of who they are. So, when you inadvertently take away your child's ownership of his learning, they are left feeling and thinking they don't know how to do it themselves. The result? They will back off and be hesitant about trying new things.

But young children learn by making mistakes and trying again. If they see an attempt as a mistake, if they think they have failed, they don't keep trying. They give up. Young children learn by doing and by figuring out how something works on their own. If given the opportunity, they will try another way at some other time until they figure it out. This is how self-initiative and excitement about learning develop.

When we as parents or other caregivers (grandparents, nannies, teachers) insist there is always a "right way," we take away the opportunity for our children to exercise independence, feel good about their choices and desires, and learn from mistakes. We also provide a clear message that their way or desire is wrong or bad. In these cases, correcting them can be the same as controlling, and both rob your child of the chance to prove he is growing and feel good about what he wants, to gain his own new skills and feel good about that, too. That's what he wants you to see and acknowledge. That's how he figures out what he can do, that his desires are valid, and that he can make choices and decisions that are valued. Toddlers are all about learning through their mistakes by figuring it out. It is the *a-ha!* moments of success when they complete something on their own (often after much trial and error) that give your child the internal excitement of *I did it!* And that is what spurs him on to want to try out more new experiences.

Have You Ever . . .

Have you ever insisted your child dress in a certain way that implies there is only one way ("the right way") to do it?

Have you ever insisted that your child write his name or letters "this way," and when he has trouble, you pick up a pencil or crayon and write it for him?

Have you ever criticized or evaluated your child's behavior or action, saying something like "that's not how you do it" or "you're doing it wrong" or "look at how your friend is doing it (different from you)"?

Even if such a correction is offered in a sweet way, your child is left feeling ashamed of her attempt or her desire to do things for herself and make her own choices. Toddlers' modus operandi is to test themselves and figure out how to do tasks on their own, in their own fashion. Choices, such as clothing, are an important part of this. They give the child feelings of knowing what she likes.

• Shaming the Compliant Child •

We all wish for an easy child. The kind who sleeps through the night at four months. Who eats well and steadily and knows when to stop. Who smiles on cue, who doesn't make a fuss in a restaurant, who plays nicely with the other children, even during the terrible twos.

Sometimes easy children are firstborn. We imagine that they had all our attention so they must have felt more secure.

Sometimes easy children come second or third. We imagine that they are easy because their older siblings were so tough and they saw how much trouble they caused in the household. In contrast, they feel like the "easy one."

Sometimes kids just seem to be born easy. More compliant. Less demanding. Less fussy. Rarely argue and never defy the parent.

Is an easy, compliant child such a good thing?

Not necessarily, if the compliance involves trying to please mom and dad, teacher or caregiver.

Sure, we want our children to listen, be responsive and respectful—but not at the expense of their very selves.

Gillian was an adorable three-year-old, whom I had known since she was eighteen months old. She was potty-trained at two. She got along well with other children. She was an all-around delightful child who was always even-tempered and well-adjusted at dropoff in the morning and later at pickup. So I was surprised when, a month after returning to the Toddler Center after the winter break, and just as she turned three years old, her mother and father told me that Gillian was having fits at home. "I don't want to go to school!" her mother repeated to me. Then the concerned mother would explain how calm, easygoing Gillian would stomp her feet in anger or fall to the floor in a heap of tears.

My first question: "Has anything at home changed?"

"Nothing," the worried mom said quickly.

I waited for a few minutes, welcomed Gillian back, and told the mom to go about her day. Maybe Gillian would let us know why she was upset. Throughout the morning, Gillian joined in the activities, played with all her usual friends, and didn't show any sign of there being something wrong or upsetting to her.

After pickup, Gillian's mom lingered for a while and then approached me.

"I've been thinking about what might be different at home. We got a new puppy about a month ago. It was Gillian's idea—she's been begging us for a dog ever since her cousins with whom she's very close got one. My husband and I thought it would be a great way to teach Gillian responsibility. And since she's an only child, we also thought a dog would be a good companion. She loves little Lulu."

I asked the mom who at home spent the most time with the new puppy, assuming (correctly it turns out) that it wasn't three-year-old Gillian who took the dog for walks, made sure the dog was fed, etc. The mom said, "Well, I do, of course."

I suggested that perhaps the reason behind Gillian's sudden fits was the situation with the new dog: On the one hand, her parents were indicating that the dog was hers to watch and care for, giving this toddler the idea that she was in charge. On the other hand, the mother was really the prime caretaker of little Lulu (just as she should be). But this left Gillian in an uncomfortable position—was she or wasn't she in charge of Lulu? And if her parents had told her that she was, but then took over the role of caretaker themselves, didn't it make sense that Gillian was upset? Confused? Even angry?

What Gillian's sudden fits and tears were telling me is that she was angry and upset, which were good, natural, understandable emotions given her predicament.

As I noted previously, all kids have negative emotions and should have negative emotions. But our so-called nice kids tend to bury or squash these negative emotions because we as adults expect them to. But when pushed to some kind of limit or extreme, like any kid these easygoing, compliant children will act out. That's normal! In fact, it is healthy.

Squashing down negative feelings such as anger, frustration, or sadness is not good for any child, but especially for the compliant child who tends to grow more and more accustomed to not having feelings. They become so attuned to their parents' perception of them as "easy," "good," or "nice," they shy away from expressing real, true feelings—some of which are bound to be negative. Whether we realize it or not, when we as adults signal to these easygoing children either our surprise or impatience when they do express frustration or upset, we only reinforce that they should not have such feelings. This means their sense of being a good or decent person is built on always being nice, saying yes, and agreeing to do whatever others want.

In another case, a young boy and his family moved overseas. The little boy was five and had been sleeping in his own bed for several years. When the family settled into their new home abroad, Adam began waking up in the middle of the night and coming into his parents' bed. The father, in particular, was very bothered by this new behavior. Without understanding the child's need for comfort and closeness, the parental response was shaming.

"You're too old to sleep in our bed," he told his son. "Your little sister is only three and she sleeps in her own bed. Why can't you?"

Ashamed and embarrassed, the boy sulked and looked away.

"I will tell you what," the mother chimed in: "If you sleep in your own bed, I will give you a gold star."

The sticker chart—a parenting tool that never does what it is meant to do. (More on that later!)

The next night, Adam woke up and went to his parents' room. In the morning, his sister, Ella, had a beautiful gold sticker next to her name; nothing was next to Adam's.

More shame and embarrassment.

After almost two weeks, long days, and even longer nights, Adam's mom called me to report what had been happening since their move and apprise me of the situation. She was upset, confused, and very sleep-deprived.

I asked about the sleeping arrangements at their new home. The mom described the town house, how the parents' master bedroom was on the second floor, while the children's rooms were above on the third floor.

I gently suggested that maybe the fact that Adam's room was on a different floor than their own was a big enough change to interrupt his sleeping routine—it certainly seemed like a big change to me.

"But Ella isn't bothered by the change," the mom said questioningly.

"But that doesn't mean Adam isn't," I said.

"Oh," the mom said, understanding.

I then suggested that she allow Adam his feelings. "Help him acknowledge that the move to a new city in a new country is a big change, and one that you will help him get familiar with. Then let him know that if he needs to come see you in the middle of the night, you will have a little bed on the floor next to your bed."

My guess was that after a few nights during which he felt

the comforting presence of his parents, he would begin to adjust to the new home and revert back to sleeping through the night in his own bed. By understanding and addressing his need, there would no longer be shame attached to the child's need for comfort.

Four mornings later, I received an ecstatic—and relieved—email from the mother. Adam was doing great! He loved his new room and was getting ready to start school. And the whole

Have You Ever . . .

Have you ever looked in astonishment or horror when your "easy child" finally acts out and hits her younger brother after he has teased her for an hour in the back of the car?

Do you constantly praise your sweet, well-behaved eldest child about how "good" and "sweet" he is?

Do you kindly second-guess the child who never gives you a hard time: "Are you sure you want to eat that second snack?" "Are you really going to wear short sleeves when it is chilly outside?"

Some children lash out, throw tantrums, and seem to have a problem with everything, nearly all the time. Other kids go silent on you; in their compliance, you may think of this sort of child as "so good," "the easy one," "what a blessing after his older brother." Danger! The too-compliant child is often the one who is so highly attuned to *your* wishes, she is suffocating her very self. The battle between wanting independence from you and wanting you to love and keep her safe forever is being won, not by her, but by you. Yes, indeed, compliance can kill the soul of a child. And when you constantly reinforce this outwardly "good" behavior, you do so often at the risk of obliterating complicated needs and feelings under the surface.

family was a lot more rested. Rather than focusing on getting him to stay in his bed, the parents accepted his need to be close to them at night. By their acknowledging the big changes of the move, addressing his negative feelings, and letting him sleep close by, his experience was validated and he felt more secure. Accepting our children for who they are and recognizing their needs allows them to move on.

Shaming by Embarrassment

Have you ever casually hinted to a teacher or another parent that your three-year-old is *still* not potty-trained, and done so right in front of him?

Have you ever reported to a friend that cute statement your child made by mixing up words, or that your daughter snuck into your bed last night, while she was within hearing?

Without realizing it, you are treating your child's developmental hiccup casually and in a way that is shaming to your child.

Shaming out of Overprotection

Have you ever held your child back from doing something, even if he might be able to, because you don't want him to get hurt? Telling him that the climber is too high when he is excited about climbing it?

Have you ever said no to a birthday party invitation of a friend because you were afraid your daughter would not have a good time?

Have you ever lied to your child about something being dangerous when it really wasn't?

Children rarely do things they can't really do. Most young

children only take the physical risks they are able to do. And if they are hesitant, they need adult support to help them move forward. Instead, our own worries and fears, about whether they will fall and get hurt, or be able to handle a social situation, get in their way. What if he is sad? What if another child won't play with him? What if she trips and skins her knee? Kids need to experience the negative in order to be able to handle it. Getting through mishaps and hard situations with their parents' support builds children's confidence ("I can handle that"). Often, parents worry so much about what the child *can't* do, they do things for them—put on their shoes, carry backpacks, feed them to be sure they get enough to eat. This only undermines children's burgeoning abilities and makes them feel bad, as in "I can't do that." The shame comes in when the parent tries to protect the child from making a mistake or doing something badly or not well; the child internalizes a sense that she is not good enough to even desire trying something new.

Shaming Through Language

Have you ever said to your child, "You're a big girl now; you don't do this anymore," when she was whiny or upset or acting younger than her age?

Have you ever used sarcasm or teased your child for so-called childish behavior? Have you ever gently reprimanded your child by calling his behavior "so silly"?

In response to our own anger, shame, or frustrations, adults use language with children that makes them feel badly, makes them feel less-than and ashamed for having a need. Instead of addressing the reason a child may be resistant to move from a crib to a big bed, we insist they should be big (denying that they also feel little). Rather than recognizing that there could be a reason the child is wildly screaming and laughing, we call them silly. Each of these diminishes the child and their feelings, leaving them with a sense of being alone and not understood. In turn, the child feels ashamed of having a need.

• The Dynamic •

As we've seen again and again in this book, children from two to five are emerging from your loving, cozy orbit in an instinctual drive to separate from you as they discover who they are and how they fit into the world around them. During this pull to become their own person, children count on you more than ever to be there when they need your comfort, reassurance, and care. It may not feel that way, but this is one of the primary paradoxes of development: In order to separate and grow into her best possible self, a child first needs a trusting relationship with you. She needs to know that she can count on you no matter what she does. This trust is built on her knowing that you understand all (or most!) of her needs. And these needs—at two, three, four, and five years old—are complicated! They are not the simple needs of an infant. The young child is in a massive mental, emotional, and social growth spurt *and* he has a very difficult time expressing all of what is going on inside of him. In fact, learning to understand all that is going on inside, and then to communicate it, is one of the biggest tasks you'll help him achieve at this age.

As she fights (because that's what it feels like to a young child—a fight!) to show you who she is, she is filled with lots of confusing and conflicting feelings and behavior. She both wants you to stay and to go. She loves you and hates you. She wants you to help her and to do it herself. She wants to laugh and to cry. It's a battle of a lifetime, a battle to become her own person.

When you fail to understand her internal struggle, her view (no matter how bizarre that view may seem), or her need of the moment, the result is a feeling of shame. Shame from the frustration of being misunderstood, or failing to please you, or not knowing what others around her seem to know.

However, when you focus on where your child is developmentally and how she is seeing the world, you will discover new insight and ways to support where they are in terms of toileting, eating, sleeping, handling emotions, managing transitions throughout the day, and other toddler tasks and goals. You can optimize these tasks for your child by avoiding shaming and honoring where your child is at the moment. The chapters in Part II will look at these aspects of daily life with toddlers and offer you examples of problems and the practical solutions to help your child internalize a growing sense of control and self-regulation, and help you keep your head on straight and actually enjoy this topsy-turvy time in your child's wondrous life!

part two

Cracking the Toddler Code

Solutions for Everyday Life

In Part I we peered into how young children develop—how they think, behave, feel, and express themselves. We explored the variations in how kids can develop at different rates and in different ways. And we especially saw how our interaction with our children at this critical time in their lives is so important to helping them—through our comfort, support, and modeling—learn to self-regulate and develop the emotional and cognitive skills necessary to truly develop fully and successfully, in a way that is best for them. With all this in mind we now turn to our individual children. How do we understand their needs and how to parent them? How do we approach the daily tasks of each day in a way that is supportive of these individual needs without losing our sense of consistency? How do our daily interactions with our children help lay the foundation for the crucial skills they need throughout their lives?

In this chapter, we will look at how to blend two points of view: meeting your child's unique needs, style, and idiosyncrasies and at the same time relying on general developmental guidelines that will help you establish boundaries and set limits to guide your young children so they develop the internal sense of security and the confidence to move out in the world. Now might be a good time to return to the questions posed in chapter 2, pages 43 to 44. These questions are meant to help you think about the unique aspects of your child and how he or she moves through the world at this point in time. By focusing on these aspects of your child right now, you will be better able to understand how they view the world and what their behaviors and actions are communicating. And keep in mind that you know your child best of all—her ins and outs, ups and downs, flash points, at any given time.

- Does he take time to warm up, or does he approach novel situations with excitement and abandonment?
- Is she determined even when she struggles with something, or does she tend to get frustrated easily?
- Does a small change in the schedule throw him off, or can he readily adjust to the different day today?

As you read through the chapters in Part II, you will always be considering how to apply these general guidelines or tips based on your child's unique set of attributes and approach to life. Your responses to those questions will likely be different today than when you pick up the book in a few months. Then again, certain characteristics of your child will stay fairly consistent. I call these the "threads" in each child—what you continue to see, at different times in their lives, expressed in new ways. My point is that, as parents, we have to keep reflecting on and cueing into who our child is, at any moment in time and in any given situation. *Is your child generally adaptable to new situations and changes in schedule? Maybe so, but not when there is a new baby in the family. A child who clings to mommy or daddy at the beginning of a birthday party? Usually, but not today when her favorite older cousin, Ted, is there, too. Doesn't like peas or corn? That was last week; this week he does.*

Consistency and change are part of every child. Knowing this will help you understand your child on a day-to-day basis, and how he is moving in the world, which will guide you in figuring out what he needs. Keep these "threads" in mind so that next time you meet the challenge of the moment (whatever that may be) you will be able to recognize both the *consistent thread*, "Jeffrey always reacts to change in routine, so of course he is upset today," and the *change* (sometimes for the better), "He was upset today, but he understood more and calmed down faster when I explained why we couldn't go to the playground after school." Dislike of change? Yes. Improved response to it? Yes. Both are at play.

Again, there is no such thing as a one-size-fits-all approach to parenting. Nurturing, supportive, loving parenting relies on your own nuanced sense of your child's needs in the day-to-day context of his or her life. Throughout Part II you will find many useful examples of how other parents handled messy situations; this variety will help you know what will work best for you and your child, while remaining calm, cool, and collected so you can meet your child's behavior with nuance, understanding, and objective guidance to create loving limits and boundaries.

Ready to go? Let's start with the need for routines, the essential structure for raising a toddler.

chapter five

Cracking the Code on Everyday Routines

Eating, Sleeping, and Toilet Training

• The Importance and Need for Routines •

Routines bring comfort. For toddlers who have no sense of time, who think tomorrow is a lifetime away and yesterday a fortnight ago, routines and regularity help children develop the flexibility and resilience they need as they grow and take on more challenges. They also act as a basis of the organization needed to develop those proven executive function skills, including planning, sequencing, and focus. I think of routines as the parentally set, practical embodiment of the limits and boundaries we are helping children internalize so that they become experts at those life skills so important to learning, socialization, and general success in life. Routines also mean repetition because they provide a structure to do something (eating, going to bed). Repetition is required for all learning and mastery; children learn and feel most comfortable when they repeat something over and over until they feel they know it well. Sameness, as bland as it may feel to adults, feels right to the toddler: "I know what I know, and that feels good."

It is yet another paradox of raising children: the more that structure and routines are in place, the freer the child is to develop the internal control to manage his or her feelings, thoughts, and behaviors—all of what enables him to mature, grow, and learn. In other words, regular routines enable flexibility. I cannot emphasize enough just how important routines are for organizing a child's days, especially when they are very young (it works for older children and teens, too, not to mention adults). Routines guide them to know what comes next, what the order is, and how to begin to manage on their own. Routines give them a sense of control because they know what to expect. Otherwise, change happens *to* them and makes them feel out of control and disoriented. A friend reported that her two-year-old was looking at picture books before bedtime, flipping from page to page. When the mom said it was time to get in his crib, the boy commented, "But I so happy now. No crib." For him, the moment consisted of the pleasure of looking at books. Moving to the crib was far from his mind. This is where falling back on an every-night (or at least most nights!) routine helps through the transition and the desire to keep the pleasure going. "I know you love your books. We can finish that book, and then it is good-night time."

Routines move children forward. At bedtime, hearing the water on in the bathtub cues them into "it is bath time," which signals to them that after bath finishes ("one more squeeze of the rubber duck and then we get out") there will be pajamas, and then teeth brushing, and then two books, two kisses, lights off, and good night. Why is this so important? Because toddlers do not organize themselves around time like we do, nor are the brain structures in place yet to organize their thoughts and actions on their own. They need our help. And routines do just that: they help toddlers sequence from one step to the next. While this helps move them toward your goal (going to sleep), it also keeps organizing their brain—every day in about the same way—to eventually take over the routine themselves (always with guidance and reminders from you). This is part of the building blocks of self-regulation.

• It's Okay to Break Routines •

While routines are important and provide organization, they do not mean we as parents have to treat every routine, every single day with rigidity. Instead, the idea is to set up basic routines that guide those tasks your children have to do daily—meals, getting dressed, leaving the house, going to sleep—which then allows for flexibility to roll with the punches when circumstances change. Routines set up a place to return to, an established order, and the comfort of familiarity. Flexibility is acquired from those times when you deviate from the routine, knowing there is the routine to return to. It is yet another paradox in parenting that routines and structure throughout the day are what enable flexibility.

For the final month of the school year, our toddler program moves to a nearby park. It is a big change, and the park is new to the children. We prepare them with a good-bye party at the center and tell them about the park. But the change still takes time to master. During the first session at the park, Irena, who had just turned three, was busily playing in the sandbox. She suddenly stopped playing, sat down on the edge of the sandbox, and announced, "I done playing. Let's go back to school now." The teacher gently reminded her that they had said good-bye to school, that it always closes in spring, and now they could play at the park. She also recognized that Irena missed the classroom. Mulling it over, Irena eventually returned to play, in spite of the changed routine. Every now and again, the little girl stopped playing, sat down, and made her statement that she was ready to go back to school. But by the second park session, the routine was clear to her; she ran to snack time before the teachers even announced it. A little routine goes a long way.

The amount of routine and help a child needs being organized varies. It varies by the child (there's that individual variation piece again!) and by what is going on in a child's life.

Take Micah, a three-year-old and firstborn child who has just started preschool. Micah loves the school calendar and comes home each day and repeats who was leader today, who will be leader tomorrow and the next day. He repeats what day it is today and will be tomorrow. He likes things in order and the routine of the calendar and his daily school "job" of announcing and keeping track of the schedule. The calendar and the idea that one day follows another, and that this order of days never changes, is comforting to him. He knows what to expect: "On Monday, Tuesday will be next. On Tuesday, I am the leader." By October, he has the routine down and is very proud of what he knows.

But then comes November. Suddenly there is no school in the middle of the week for Veterans' Day. But he has just begun to learn that school happens on each day of the week—and is able to rattle off that information—"Monday, Tuesday, Wednesday, Thursday, and Friday, I go to school. On Saturday and Sunday I don't go to school. Mommy and Daddy stay home, too."

Suddenly his mother's proclamation that there is no school even though it's Tuesday stuns little Micah.

Micah starts to sob, screaming between the tears, "Yes, school. Today is Tuesday. Tuesday is school!!" Micah had been very used to his routine, and to the orderliness that it brought to his day and week. And then suddenly, just as he felt in control of it all, this sudden change appears. It is too much for him.

This kind of illogical change can be very confusing for young children, particularly for a child like Micah who thrives on routines and establishing order. Some children are more flexible than others, but for Micah, keeping things in order—whether it is school days or the precise lineup of his toy cars—is a priority (at least at this age), so he falls apart. Similarly, he can focus long and attentively on putting together his train track following a very specific order and arrangement of the pieces. Yet, as you can probably guess, if a piece is out of order, he will collapse in a tantrum and yell to his mother, "Fix it! Fix it! It's broken!!"

After a repeated number of such instances, his mother came to me very concerned about her son. She asked, "Is something wrong with Micah?"

Of course not. In fact, I pointed out to her, Micah's reliance on order can be a good quality later: he gets an idea into his head of how things should be and he works to make sure that what he has envisioned happens. In an older child or adult we'd see this trait as persistence, one of those skills that enable a stick-to-itiveness so important to problem solving and academic and other kinds of life success. (Plus, over time, with brain development and experience, he will develop increased flexibility.)

But I also explained to this worried mom that right now, at this developmental stage, Micah was lacking the ability to understand that it's okay to break a routine or vary the arrangement of the train track. He had not yet developed this flexibility. At his young age, he is not rational enough to understand changes, including that this Tuesday is different because it's a holiday. And his brain could not yet switch modes to accommodate this change. In time, with her guidance and reminders, he'll get to be more flexible. Is this true of all three-year-olds? No. For some children more than others, responding to change and being flexible takes more work on the parents' part. But it does not mean something is wrong with them. They just need more guidance for now.

Some children become undone by breaks in routines. Others bounce back fairly quickly. A few barely seem to notice any changes. In time, nearly all children become more flexible with routines. The worry and upset that children feel at these moments of disrupted routine stem from losing a sense of comfort. Routines bring them a security that they know what to expect; they know what comes next and find comfort in knowing the established order. They feel in control and can relax and feel assured that all is well. Then, suddenly, the rules change! It is a shock, even if the change feels minor to you. Change can actually be frightening or disorganizing to the child. *Where did my sense of order and knowing what is happening go?* The ground feels unsteady.

A mother reported that the previous night, her four-year-old refused to go to sleep. Bedtime, which usually took thirty minutes and then lights out, lasted over two hours. He asked for more water, he had to use the bathroom again, he requested she stay, he cried, he came out of his room. He pulled out every trick he could and would not go to sleep. I tried to figure out with the mother what was going on at home, or at school, that may have been bothering him. Nothing. Any changes? Visitors? Upcoming events? Nothing. Changes to his routine? Nothing. Suddenly she paused and thought of something that had seemed so minor but she now realized was not. "Every night after his books I sing him a lullaby and we have a quick good-night ritual. But last night I really wanted to watch this show with my husband. I had gotten home from work late and was rushing through bedtime so I could have my grown-up time. In my rush, I forgot to sing the lullaby and do our nightly ritual." That was what threw him off. Bedtime returned to thirty minutes *and* included the lullaby.

Does this mean that every parent should follow the same thirty-minute prescription? Not at all. You help to establish the routine that works for *your* child. Sometimes parents try to "hide" the change in routine by not mentioning it, pretending it did not happen and hoping the child won't notice. This approach can backfire. Even if a child handles it at the time, they often fall apart later. It's best to be straightforward and direct.

What to Do

So what can a parent do in these situations when the routines are altered? Maybe a relative is in town, or school is closed for teacher meetings. Maybe the TV or iPad is broken and your child is not going to watch *Sesame Street* before going to preschool. Helping your child through these smaller changes sets your child up for handling bigger changes and stressors throughout life. How do you handle changes without walking on eggshells (which is how many parents feel) worrying that your child will fall apart?

First, recognize that your child may not like the change in routine, and that it is your job to guide and reassure them through the upset. You know the change is temporary and will be okay after all; convey that to the child. This approach also builds trust in your child—they learn that they can count on you to tell them what is going on (even if they don't like it) and that you will help them.

For known changes: Explain what is coming before it happens, but not too far in advance. "Today when you wake up, Grandma will be here. I have to go to work early so Grandma came to take care of you. I will be home for dinner and see you then." Children don't necessarily like these changes, even when prepared, so it is important to recognize the disappointment. "You may not like this, but tomorrow [Tuesday] is a funny day. Usually you have school on Tuesdays. But this Tuesday will be different—a no-school day."

For unexpected changes: There will certainly be times of unanticipated change. And this is where your comforting and supportive response comes into play even more. I recall taking one of my kids to preschool when he was four. It was a warm spring day, after a rainy week, and the teachers had decided to start the morning on the roof play deck, something they had not done before. We arrived at school to this news. Not good news as far as my son was concerned: he froze in his tracks with a blank expression, then quietly started to cry. His routine was off and for a child who always wanted to know (and still does) what to expect, he didn't like it. I imagine he was thinking, *Wait! I know the routine, I know what to do when I arrive at school. All was well. Whose dumb idea was this to change it?!*

The teacher immediately recognized his worry about the change and reassured him that the teachers would still take care of him, and that there would be inside playing later, too. To help him through the sudden change, I accompanied them up to the roof and showed him that his teachers and friends were there. Then, each morning for the next week we discussed what type of a day it was—an inside day or a roof day. Eventually he adjusted to handling good-bye, wherever the day started. Changes happen.

Parents Have Trouble Breaking Routines, Too

I have found over the many years of working with parents that adults, too, can get thrown off by changed routines. So, if a parent worries about being flexible in the routine, you can be sure that the child picks up on this nervousness. Flexibility comes when parents can reassure their children that a change is temporary and soon they will return to what they are used to ("Today we are having a picnic lunch and eating outside. That's different. But tonight you will still get to sit in your seat at home"). Many parents overly worry that a break in their child's routine will be ruinous. Maybe they worked hard to get their child to bed without battle, so they are afraid that getting home late one night will throw the whole thing off. Or they decline an offer to meet a friend visiting from out of town because it means eating lunch later than usual, and "my child needs her schedule."

As director at the Barnard Toddler Center for nearly two decades, the most common question I get from parents prior to the start of a new school year is "How can I do an afternoon class if my child naps? He naps at exactly the same time every day." I have this conversation many times each summer. Some parents turn down the program if they are offered an afternoon group, even if it is only one day a week, because they are afraid of changing naptime. My sympathetic response to parents? Children adapt. I had the same concerns with my own children when they attended in the afternoon, but they were far more flexible than I knew. Some children skip their nap that day, but still nap on other days. Other children take a shorter, but earlier nap, on school days. But one thing I know for sure: parents have a harder time adjusting to the change in nap routine than any toddler does.

• Routines: Sleeping, Toileting, and Eating •

Sleep

We live in a sleep-deprived society; children do not get enough sleep. While there is a range of how much sleep each child needs, one thing is certain: managing behavior and handling life's ups and downs are much easier when a child (and adult!) is well rested. And like everything else we have been discussing in this book, there is variability in how well children handle sleep. Some are naturally better regulated when it comes to sleep: they easily sleep through the night, they fall asleep quickly, and they wake rested and balanced. Other children need more help. How much sleep a child needs varies as well. Some fortunate parents have children who sleep twelve or more hours a night. Others are fine with nine hours. Some nap two to three hours by day, others forty-five minutes. Some are early morning risers (in spite of everything a parent tries, they can be up and ready to go at 5:30 A.M.); others sleep until 8 A.M. These are likely inborn ways of your child. However, all children need enough sleep (whatever their amount is) and a good night of rest. Parents play a significant role in building good sleep habits; it is one of the biggest gifts we can give our children.

Getting a child to sleep and helping her to sleep on her own or through the night can be taxing to everyone involved. To understand issues in sleep, let's go back to the main developmental task of this age: separation. As I mentioned earlier, at the Barnard Toddler Center our focus is on separation. We think of sleep as the final separation of the day for the child, which means the crux of sleep-related challenges has to do with separation anxiety. Not only is sleep about separation, it also is the longest separation of the day (for nine to thirteen hours). While adults may love doing it (and wish we had more hours for sleeping), often kids this age don't. Bedtime occurs when they are the most tired, have the least resources, and are in the dark, most likely alone, and for an extended number of hours. Parents don't often think of sleep as separation, but from the child's point of view that's what it is. Another good-bye. Thinking of it this way can help you reframe bedtime routines and limits to ensure that everyone gets a full night's sleep. Daytime behaviors are much improved when everyone gets sleep!

Sleep can be affected by changes in your child's life. Did she recently start school? Is mommy traveling for work? Is daddy working longer hours than usual? Has your daughter developed new skills or is she on the verge of a developmental leap forward (which you only know in retrospect)? Is there tension in the house, or are you expecting a new baby? Is she just getting over a cold? Any change, large or small, can impact how a child sleeps. Emotions can affect her, too. Did you have a battle of the wills with him today? Or was he generally out of sorts? Any of these emotions can alter sleep as anxieties come seeping out at night. Suddenly the child awakens and screams, "Mommy!" when before he might have just turned over and gone back to sleep.

During the start of our program each fall, when toddlers are just beginning the school year, parents will report a range of sleep disruptions for some children. One parent noted, "She comes to school so well, says good-bye with a big smile, and is happy to play here. I am relieved she doesn't cry when I leave. I don't know why, but she used to sleep through the night, and now she awakens most nights calling for me." In this case, the child may have mastered the separation by day, to her mother's delight, but the intense emotions of it are coming out at night. Be careful what you wish for!

Bedtime is also about limit setting, holding up the guidelines so your child can master a restful night of sleep. If you find that it is hard to say no or set limits for your child by day, then bedtime can be particularly problematic. If you are negotiating a lot with her by day, giving in rather than holding limits, bedtime will be hard. Children need our loving help to set up and reinforce a routine and limits, so that they can successfully separate at night. I find that parents can have a hard time setting limits at bedtime based on their own history. Do you remember wishing your parents would stay with you at bedtime but they would not? Did you feel like you needed more than your parents could provide in terms of comfort, even outside of bedtime? Did you feel overlooked in a large family and without the reassurances you needed? Were you awake at night, scared or anxious? Are you currently a poor sleeper or worrier in the late hours of the night? If so, you are not alone in these feelings, but it may be hard for you to set a limit for your child, fearing that you will be letting him down. Think about your own issues around sleep and separation; disentangling your own feelings will make you a better support for your child.

One mother whose three-and-a-half-year-old rarely went to sleep on her own bemoaned, "If I leave her room before she is sound asleep—which can take up to two hours!—my daughter screams, 'I need you! I need you!' It makes me feel so bad. I just can't bear it and I go back. I am the youngest. My parents were always pushing me to go to bed on my own. If I asked them to stay with me, they got irritated. And I would feel terrible. I don't ever want to do that to her. I'm afraid she'll be mad at me, too."

In fact, this mother was doing the same thing to her child, even though she was understandably frustrated with her. Often, identifying the trigger can be enough to move a parent to change responses. Soon after making the connection to her childhood, this mom decided to set a limit and be consistent in her own behavior at bedtime, realizing, "Even if she is mad at me, she'll be fine by the morning. And we'll all sleep better." She told her daughter that it was okay if the child missed her at night, that she'd still see her in the morning. She gave her a handkerchief that the mother usually carried and told the child she could sleep with it to be reminded of the mother all night. Then she told her it was okay to cry, mommy would be back in the morning, no matter what. It took a few nights, but the mother stuck to her plan. And with that, bedtime got easier. Why? Because the mother was clear with her child (and herself) about the limits and need for sleep; children respond to our cues.

Another mother, who was working long hours at a new job, commented about her son's middle-of-the-night awakenings. "I feel so guilty that I am not home more with him. When he wakes up screaming for me I feel like, well, I can't let him down now. He sees so little of me." After helping her identify these feelings and see the connection to his sleep problems, she worked out coming home a half hour earlier each day. She felt less guilty by not being so rushed at home. This allowed them more time together for dinner and in the evening, and the sleep issues stopped. Once again, children respond to the actions of the parents.

Our own feelings as parents can interfere with what our children really need from us, and for this reason being attuned parents means cueing in not only to the needs of our children but to our own feelings and past experiences.

What To Do: Bedtime Routine

It will not surprise you that successful bedtimes require routine, routine, routine. The routine cues your child in to the steps leading up to going to sleep, and helps him wind down in a gradual manner. Establish a routine that happens at about the same time each night, in the same order (basically!) to help his body habituate to timing for sleep. Bedtime routines should be calm, comforting, and relaxing. Think of the routine as going from the active pace of day to more and more calm, so that by the time she is in bed or her crib, she has settled

Tovah's Tips for Bedtime Routine

- Monitor baths: For some children bathtime winds them up. If that is the case, do it earlier in your routine, or leave it for the morning. For others, it is calming.
- Avoid electronics and TV, which can have a reawakening effect on many children. They seem calm and cozied in as they watch TV, but then they are excited when the video is done. Best not to use electronics or TV close to bedtime.
- Keep routines short and simple. They should take no more than an hour (at most, if you are including the bath), and thirty minutes is even better. Lengthier routines get children stirred up as they have extra time to anticipate the inevitable separation.
- Let them have simple choices. "Would you like to read *Curious George* first or *Goodnight Moon*?" Such simple questions give them some, but limited control and keeps you moving forward to bed.
- Sing or listen to a lullaby—either can be soothing. Some parents like to add prayers or a quiet review of the day.
- Try to create a cozy corner in their room for sleep once your child moves to a bed. Make sure the bed is against a wall, ideally in a corner, and feels like a comforting place.
- If one parent is coming home late, do your best not to have it during the good-night routine. For many children, the return of that parent stirs them up. Better that they see you, when they are refreshed, in the morning.

into a low-key state, ready for sleep. When my children were young, I'd dim their bedroom light after bath when we entered to put on pajamas. I could see them cue in to the start of the winding-down routine. As we sat down to read books, lights low, I'd turn on the air filter that hummed quietly as white noise, and just as the books were finishing, I'd start their lullaby music. Then we'd do snuggles and kisses on each cheek before saying good night.

The details of the routine vary by family. The important thing is that children thrive on a simple set of rituals that are followed nightly. Especially for two- and three-year-olds, who will get more flexible at four and five, the same routine—including books, lullaby, kisses and snuggles, or whatever your ritual is—is important to prepare them for sleep.

Sleep Challenges

Extra Rituals

Some children need to create a clear ritual of their own before they go to bed—rearranging their toys or stuffed animals in an exact, meticulous order; picking out the precise items to take to bed with them; or lining up their cars or dolls in a particular way. Others sleep with the same lovey every night. A mother sent me a photo of her toddler asleep with five blankets, which he insisted be rolled up and surrounding him, and ten small teddy bears he carefully arranged. He slept soundly in the middle of them. If your child needs certain items in a certain order, as mine did, give her the time to do it, as long as they do not get carried away with delaying bedtime. This may mean starting bedtime five or ten minutes earlier. For some children, this organizing ritual helps them settle down and feel calm before saying good night.

Stall Tactics

Be mindful of stall tactics, those pleas of "one more book;" "I need water;" "I have to pee-pee;" "Can I tell you one more thing, Mommy!! Um, um, I love you." I don't consider them "manipulative," as parents often report. These are all ways to put off the impending separation. The best way to handle these attempts to stall good night is to indulge them a little, knowing the reason for it, but with *clear* boundaries. "Pick two more things to do and then we will say good night. I'll see you in the morning." Or, if you know what the stall tactics are, address those needs prior to getting into bed: "Let's get your water. Now be sure to make pee-pee. Here is your bunny and blankie, right where you like them. I am going to give you three last kisses and then say good night!" And yes, it is fine to ignore the continued requests and to be loving and clear about your limit (as in, "I'll see you tomorrow!").

When you are serious about being done, your child picks up on that and responds. But I promise you this: if you are hesitant and feeling badly about saying good night or like you are abandoning them, they will sense that and keep pushing for that "one more thing." They'll be overtired, you'll get frustrated, and no one will feel rested in the morning.

Night Awakenings

Children wake up at night for a variety of reasons, just like older children or adults. Some children are better about getting back to sleep than others. Children sometimes call out for you, but if you wait, they typically fall back asleep. Wait and see if they do. Other children wake up crying, either from nightmares or unknown reasons, and may need your reassurance to settle back down. The key is to keep your response calm and brief as possible—lights off and talk as little as you can (it arouses them), and simply rub their back or comfort them physically, a little bit, just enough to let them know they are okay.

Nightmares can be scary, especially when your child wakes up screaming. They are the fears or anxieties of the day flowing out in their sleep. A nightmare now and then is normal at these ages and happens at some point for nearly every child as they learn to handle negative feelings, control urges and impulses, deal with new babies at home, or transition to school and master independence, including toilet training. So if your child awakens upset from a nightmare, they will need your comfort. Reassure her by simply saying, "I am here. It's okay. You had a dream." You may have to remind her, "You had a bad dream. That is over now; it is not real. Now you are okay, mommy [or daddy] is here. You can go to sleep now." Toddlers can't distinguish real from pretend, so your child may need your reassurance that the scary thing in the dream is not real. In other words, provide reassurance and calm, in a low-key way.

I find that often parents talk to their children—ask them questions, if they are okay, what is wrong, and so on. Of course this is our parental instinct. But engaging your child this way wakes them up more and arouses them. Instead, what they need is your calming presence, your assurance that the dream is not real and can't hurt them, and for you to put them back to sleep.

You may wonder why your child is suddenly having nightmares, especially if she never had them before. It has to do with her developmental stage. As she becomes more verbal, her imagination grows along with it. By day he may imagine the good things—"I am Superman!" "I am cooking pancakes for my daddy"—but he can also imagine the bad things—monsters, fires, mean dogs with big teeth, mommy or daddy leaving him. The fears, anger, and worries of the day spill into their sleep and dreams. "If I can get this angry at Mommy or Daddy then could they get this angry at me?" Nightmares are common and normal in this age group, starting after age two and for some children continuing well beyond. One of mine used to bolt into my room, at two or three in the morning, his heart pounding, breathing fast. I knew he'd had a bad dream. Sometimes he would cry. What he needed was to snuggle for several minutes until he settled down. I could feel his breathing return to normal, his body relax. I'd carry or walk him back to bed, kiss him, and he'd be sound asleep soon. Another one of mine needed me to hold and rock him in my arms as I assured him the dream could not hurt him, until he'd reach for his bed, a signal he was ready to get back into it. The whole thing took less than five minutes.

Nightmares can initially frighten a parent, especially if they have never heard their child screaming in the middle of the night. Not to worry: having fears, anger, and worry is part of the desperate pull to become their own person. Too bad it disrupts sleep!

If your child is awakening nightly, help her to sleep through the night by giving her something of yours to sleep with—a T-shirt, a handkerchief, or even a small pillow. Also give her a family photo. Say to your child, "Here is Mommy's (Daddy's) shirt. You can hold on to it all night for me. And if you miss me, it is here, and so is our family." It is a way of keeping you close throughout the night. Children feel better once they return to sleeping through the night—a triumph of independence as well as being better rested. Not all children will accept a substitute for you, but simply the gesture of offering it says to them, "I am here for you, even at night."

But what if your child is having nightmares multiple nights a week? In this case, think about what is going on in her life. Although nightmares are a response to their daytime life, they don't usually occur every night. Is your child resisting toilet training? It may be time to back off. Is your child being exposed to TV shows that are scary for him (even if they don't seem scary to adults or his older sibling)? Are you talking too much about their new school, which is still a month away? Do a review of what is going on and try to bring stressors down.

Night Terrors

Night terrors, which are different from nightmares, occur in a small percentage of children. They usually happen earlier in their sleep cycle and are often on nights when they are overtired (sleep-deprived, out of routine, on vacation, out of town visitors, etc.). While living through one can be quite upsetting to the parents, they are of no harm to the child. At first, you may think your child is having a nightmare. The difference is that your child is not in an awake state. They are asleep, in fact, in a deep sleep that they most often cannot be awakened from. Because of this, they can be screaming and thrashing with their eyes wide open. They may be calling for you, and even though you are there, they do not know that, so they may scream at you or for you to go away.

The whole episode can feel terrible to the parent, but your child will not even remember the episode (since they are asleep)—unless, of course, you keep asking him in the morning about it and he feels like he has to make something up to please you! My advice is to not say anything about it. Usually, after thrashing and screaming, the child falls back into a deep sleep, as if nothing occurred. The night terror can last five minutes or thirty. The important thing is that your child is kept safe so he can't accidentally pull or knock something over. Some children will let you hold them; others will push away and get more upset if touched. Your best option is to wait for it to pass and find a way to reassure yourself. The first two times my son had a night terror (before I knew what it was) were among my scarier nights.

When to Move Your Child from a Crib to a Bed

As toddlers move out into the world to explore, there is much to discover. It is a big world filled with good things and bad—managing new feelings and impulses, trying to please mommy and daddy by using the potty and not throwing toys, growing imaginations conjuring up good and bad. There is a lot to fear out there. Cribs provide children with a safe and cozy place where they can unwind and be cozied in on all sides in a small space. And yet, in this hyperparenting climate today, parents are often eager to move their children to the next step. I strongly urge parents to resist this when it comes to the crib. Before the age of three, most children feel the safety of the crib as a comfort and relief. Taking them out too early sets them up to have to manage a great deal of freedom (I can get out on my own! Nothing to keep me in bed!) before they may be ready. Better to err on the older side (after age three). You are giving them the gift of a secure place at the end of the day when they don't have to work on controlling their impulses (as in working to stay in bed!).

Parenting POV

Do I Let My Child Cry at Night?

This is a question I get often. Since there are so many books out there espousing different methods for helping your child learn to sleep on his or her own, some beginning at four to six months old, I feel the need to weigh in here. As you've probably picked up, sleep issues don't miraculously disappear once your child moves from infancy to toddlerhood. First, cue in to that particular child's needs. Second, think about any sleep issue (trouble going to sleep, staying asleep, or fear of sleeping alone) as a separation issue. Third, reassure your child at night if they are scared or worried, and establish a routine (see page 107). They need your comfort, but with limits. Sleep is a piece of independence, and children feel proud when they can handle it on their own.

But some children need your help getting there. If the disruptions turn into a nightly happening and there is nothing else wrong (child has fever, is sick, or there is another problem), a limit needs to be set. Children count on us to establish these limits. Your child will feel better, and so will you. Learning to sleep on one's own is an important accomplishment. When we deprive them of this accomplishment because of our own worries—*Am I letting my child down? Will she be mad at me? What if I am missing her need?*—we are actually hindering their march toward independence. No one can tell you to let your child cry unless you are okay with it. But I can assure you of this: children this age gain trust when they learn that it is okay to cry, even at night, and mommy and daddy still love them. It shows them, once again, you are there for them, no matter how hard something feels. Why? Because you have helped them get over a tough hurdle and they feel safer that way. You get my point—a good night's sleep benefits everyone!

• Toileting •

I must admit this is not my favorite topic. Why? Think about it: who (other than five-year-olds who do a lot of potty talk about "poopy-poopy, you are poopy" and teens who enjoy discussions of flatulence) wants to talk about bathroom habits? No, really. Like anything else that your child eventually masters, including separation, sleeping through the night, and giving up bottles, the lead-up to it is often exaggerated and can make the task even harder. They all get out of diapers, if we give them the guidance, take the pressure off, throw our worries, expectations, and own embarrassment aside, and ignore the advice of so many well meaning relatives. ("Oh, darling, you were toilet trained before two and never had an accident.")

Believe me, your child *knows* you want them to use the toilet. That is clear to any toddler. *The grown-ups are happier when I use the toilet.* Ultimately, your child wants to please you and fulfill this wish of yours. And I can promise you they will. One day. Just not necessarily on your timetable and definitely not if your child feels pressured. The flip side of the pressure to leave their diapers behind before they are ready is shame. Why? Because using the toilet is a very personal and intimate act. It also triggers fears for many toddlers. "If poopy comes out, what else can fall off, too?" Really. I know it sounds odd, but remember that their brains think differently than ours do. "Will Mommy be so mad at me if I don't do it? If I have an accident? Will Daddy think I am bad?" This is the response to being pushed before they are ready to commit to this.

Like so many tasks during these years, giving up diapers is a step toward independence. This is an especially big one, and it balances out the independence ("I wear underpants now, just like Daddy and Mommy and my big brother!") with the fear of losing control. Remember that toddlers are all about being in control. This is one act they need to control for themselves. Learning to use the toilet is complicated, and for some children more difficult to master than others.

So my first advice is to back off. Hold yourself back from any strong efforts to get them out of diapers before they are ready (believe me, I was ready to be done with diapers, too, in my house, but I promised myself I would not push it, and it turned out to be much easier).

On the other side, getting out of diapers is another step for your child toward independence and creates a good feeling of "I did it! I feel good!" That is the incentive they eventually have, and in truth, they don't want to keep letting you down. So, in time, when they show an interest and that they are ready, they will need your support and guidance. But as with every step toward independence, you want to keep power struggles out of it.

So many parents spend precious time and energy fretting about toilet training when we all know that every single child will get toilet trained. When the pressure is off, and there is a little potty that sits in the bathroom, then with even a little structure and encouragement, and lots of reminders, it happens. Do your best not to get worked up about this, even when it feels like your child is just too old for diapers, or you think is the only one wearing them (I assure you that is not the case). You will only get your child more anxious. And remember, you can expect a few (or many) accidents along the way—two steps forward and one step back.

What to Do

- Stay calm. They are looking to you for cues, so if you are worked up and nervous, they will mimic those feelings. Monitor your feelings about this to keep them away from your child. Many parents have mixed emotions, ready to be done with diapers but sad to lose the baby. Know your own thoughts and feelings first.
- Be encouraging but not overzealous. Don't overdo the prizes, stickers, or treats. Using the toilet is *their* accomplishment, and prizes or bribes make it about you, not them. Think about it: They will use the toi-

let every day, many times, for their entire life going forward. Do you want them to expect a parade or candy each time?! Their own pride and excitement is what carries them forward with the toilet training. And the smile on your face or hug is a reward in and of itself. At the same time, don't ever punish them for having an accident or refusing to use the potty. This will cause shame and set the process backward.

- Pick a time with relative calm, not when they are starting a new school, changing babysitters, or a new baby is in the family. I find that warm weather is easiest (fewer and lighter clothes, and it's easier to carry changes of clothes and handle soiled ones). Pick a two-week window when you can focus on it with them (so not a time with visitors, or with a big work task ahead).
- Buy underwear. They may even like to try it on. Let them know that "tomorrow we will be all done with the diapers and you can wear underpants." Don't do this more than a day in advance, since it creates too much anxiety. And certainly don't ask for agreement, as in "Would you like to stop wearing diapers tomorrow?" Toddlers are not ones for keeping a promise anyhow. The promise is for this moment only, and tomorrow is a new day. Toddlers love to run around naked, which can help in the toilet-training process. Yes, they will go on the floor, so be ready for that. But it helps them understand the process (and have fun being naked!).
- Help them put on the underwear, in a clear and matter-of-fact manner. Then, for the first couple of

weeks (or longer for some children), you will have to regularly take them to the toilet. No need to ask; the answer will be no. Remember—independence also means power and control. Instead, set up a schedule for yourself, or your caregiver. For example: when child wakes up, after breakfast, an hour later, etc. Give your child a heads-up. "First we'll eat lunch and then I'll take you to the potty." You will have to take them and stay with them. It should be a fun time. Some children like to look at a book or have you tell a story. It is fine if they don't go, just say, "You sat on the potty and nothing came out. That happens sometimes. We'll try again later." No praises, no reprimands. A quick hug when they jump off the potty reassures them all is still well.

- Use a stool under their feet or a toddler potty. Many children are afraid to sit on the toilet—it is way high up, their feet dangle, and they feel as if they will fall in. A potty on the floor feels safer to most.
- Accept that accidents are going to happen. If your child has an accident (which she will!), make no big deal of it. Explain, "Oh, that is the pee-pee. Sometimes it comes out. Let's get changed." Disposable diapers are so absorbent that often toddlers are surprised that the pee-pee makes them wet. This is part of the learning. Even if your toddler sails through the toilet training, he may have an accident weeks (or months) into it. Expect it to happen, and then you won't be taken aback when it occurs.
- Back off if your child seems to be fighting getting out of his or her diaper. They may just not be ready—for whatever reason. It is fine to go back

to diapers (*no shaming*), and tell them, "Diapers are fine. We'll try again another time." Then reassure them that you love them whether they wear underpants or diapers. When parents back off and don't care one way or the other what the child uses (diapers or toilet), the child often announces she is ready to use the potty. The catch is that you have to be genuine.

- Nighttime bedwetting is common in many children long past the time they are dry during the day. Being dry at night can come months or years later and all children get there eventually, just not on a parent's desired timeline. Toddlers can stay in diapers or pull-ups at night. Don't make a big deal out of this and assure them that this is fine. Children take their cues from parents so if you are not bothered by the wetting (no need to be, it's normal) they will not be. Some children sleep deeply, others do not yet have the signal at night to wake up. You can try taking your child to the bathroom before you go to sleep, which works for some but not for all. My advice to you is back off, be relaxed about this, and never shame a child who wets the bed. If your child wets occasionally and sleeps in underwear, put extra sheets on the bed, with a waterproof pad in between and dry pajamas nearby. That way, you can quickly strip the wet layer, change the wet pajamas, and everyone is back to sleep quickly! But if you are still concerned, speak to your pediatrician.

• Food and Eating •

Everyone knows at least one picky eater. Why? Because kids this age tend to be that way! You may even have a picky eater in your house right now. Some children are picky in general, maybe eating only white foods like bread and pasta, or only certain textures or flavors. Some insist on the exact same lunch being packed every day for preschool, five days a week. It may be boring for you but for your child the same daily meal every day when she opens her lunch brings comfort. Others go through phases of being pickier. Remember their drive to show their independence? Food is another place they can play out a growing sense of their own power. "Do I eat this like Mommy wants me to? Do I really even like it? Do I *have* to eat it?" This is all part of their new level of independence and decision making, as in "I *don't* like that!" These opportunities give them the feeling of control.

Most children like to eat and are frequently hungry, but they can have strong reactions to new and different foods—especially vegetables! This is where the desire to control comes into play. As your child becomes more aware of being her own person, she also wants to make choices. Independence and becoming her own person mean recognizing choices and exerting her own will. Food is one of the few places in their daily life where children can enforce control (so are using the toilet, choosing clothes, and going to sleep). I have a child who ate only Cheerios, every dinner, for almost a year. We'd start dinner with his regular meal then he'd remember, "I only want Cheerios for dinner." Not just any cereal; only Cheerios would do. It was all about his choosing his meal, him being "in control" and exerting his power. Then he started eating a more regular range of foods again, and as a much bigger child he eats a wide variety. But he still loves cereal, all kinds now!

Toddlers are capable of feeding themselves, although they use hands to augment the utensils. We live in a health-conscious time (which can be good) and parents worry a lot about what their children eat and how much. They worry that they don't eat enough, or not enough of the right things, or that they don't know when to stop. Believe me, none of our grandparents (and probably parents, too) noticed what we ate. They served it; we ate. For us as parents, feeding our children is an act of love, but it can also become a place of control on our part. "Two more bites," "carrots first and then you can have bread," "don't you want more? You can't possibly be full." In truth, this approach undermines our children's attempts to develop good eating habits.

Like nearly every parent, I believe in healthy eating. But the bottom line is that only the child knows if she is hungry or full, and when you force them to eat (as in "one more bite"), your child cannot learn to trust her own hunger signals. Parents tend to see mealtimes as all about food. Here is another way to think of mealtimes—as social times. Use this time to sit with your children (not that we can all do this seven nights a week!), chat about the day, and be together as a family. Often it can't be all of you, but at least one adult (parent, babysitter, grandparent) should be sharing in the meal (at least sipping something), eating and chatting but not noticing what the child is or is not eating. If the eating routine is relaxed (or as relaxed as eating with toddlers can be!) and enjoyable, then children will eat well on their own.

Parents often come to me worried that their picky eaters are not getting enough nourishment. I ask first if their pediatrician is concerned. The answer is almost always no. So unless your pediatrician is concerned about your child's nutrition, I don't think you need to be. And yet, out of parental love and their own feelings or anxiety about food, or the idea that being a good parent includes feeding a child a certain amount of food, they might resort to chasing after a defiant three- or four-year-old with a spoon or making promises they don't want to keep ("If you eat two more bites of broccoli, you can have ice cream"), or shoveling in a few more spoonfuls. This is another place where our own history can mold our interactions with our children. Were you a fat kid? A picky eater? Was mealtime fraught with tension or fighting as a child? Do you recall people making comments about what you did or did not eat? All of this can affect your attitude about food for your child and your response to their eating.

Now that you know about your child's drive for independence, take a step back for a moment and think about what these actions feel like to him. Remember, they are striving for power and control and to show you all they can do "by myself." That includes eating, from deciding how much they will eat to feeding themselves. Each time we bribe or cajole them to eat or make one food contingent on another (finish the chicken and I will give you cake), we give them a message that counters all they are trying to achieve. The message they hear is: you don't know what is best for yourself, only I do. And this is where battles come in.

Instead of engaging in these conflicts, think of eating and mealtime at these ages as setting up good eating habits now for your child to carry through as they get older and can make healthy, independent choices—to know when they are hungry or not. You don't want food to be a battleground or associated with anxiety and negative emotions. If it is, once on their own, you can be sure they won't be able to make good choices. As a mother of now-older children, I can say that before you know it, they are eating at friends' houses or making their own snacks or meals. Setting up good eating habits young is the way to help them make reasonable independent eating choices later. In fact, nutritionists say that controlling children's eating backfires; later on they rebel or sneak food, or don't know how to read hunger signals and don't feel equipped to make good decisions around food. What your child eats over a seven- to ten-day period is what matters, not what they eat at any one meal or day.

What to Do

I truly believe mealtimes can be pleasant, even with toddlers. But it all starts with us. For parents mealtimes take patience, a steady, routine approach, and recognition that toddlers are learning. That likely means changing your expectations about what mealtimes will be. Good-bye to the leisurely or romantic meals of pre-children. By taking control battles out of eating, giving limited options, and making mealtime a social occasion, you can help your child become a good (or even great) eater. Maybe not today, but it does happen.

- Sit at a table for all meals. Children need structure to learn the eating routine, and the table defines the space. It shows them that mealtime is a time where we sit and eat, and there is no wandering. Food is eaten at a table. For young children, eating with a TV or iPad on is a distraction. Mealtime is just that—for meals. And that means food and socializing—no outside entertainment required.
- Sit mostly in the same seats. Toddlers enjoy the sameness of sitting in the same spot at the table and counting on where others sit, too. This becomes their routine. As you know, an exact order to things brings comfort. Having a regular seat makes the meal ritual easier to follow.

- Sit with them, eat a little. You may not want to eat at five or five thirty or in the midst of the mess the toddler creates. Understandable. But because it is a social event, and because they learn the routine from the adults, even if you are not eating your main meal with them it is important you sit with them and nibble on something light. How could they possibly know, over time, how to act at meals unless it is modeled, over and over again? They will model your behavior and learn that meals are social times. "Mommy sits for dinner, Daddy sits for dinner, we talk, I do, too." If you are not home, another parent, nanny, grandparent, or other adult eating with them is fine.
- Talk about anything *except* the food. The idea is to socialize your child in mealtime behavior and that means not paying attention to the food they eat. For some parents this is a hard shift to make. But think about how it would feel to you if your friends commented on how much you ate of a meal. Or maybe you remember your own parent shaming you: "You don't like that? Why'd you eat so little?" Children actually eat more when no one notices or comments on what they are eating (remember, it is not what they eat at every meal that matters; it is what they eat over the course of a week or so).
- Chat about the day, or what they will be doing on the weekend or something related to them. "I was thinking about when we were at the park. Do you remember the dog we saw? He was barking loudly." You can also ask what they recall, especially as they get older. This type of conversation makes mealtime enjoyable and helps them learn how to be in the

company of others. In the meantime, they eat with no focus on the food. In other words, do all you can *not* to notice what they eat. At the same time, don't expect your young child to always engage in the conversation. You may be doing more of it for a while.

- When your child is done eating, she is done. Most children, especially at two and three, won't sit once they are finished and it is not reasonable to expect them to. It should be fine for them to get up and go play. Say to them, "You know if you are full. If you are done, you can go play. Dinner is finished." This helps them learn hunger and full signals and says that you trust them to know when they've had enough. But you also mean business. Sit to eat. Up means done. Throwing food? That is a signal he is finished and you can interpret it as just that. "I see you are finished eating. You can get down now." Remove their plate so they understand what you mean. If they have just started eating, I suggest trying "We don't throw food. If you are done, I can take your plate," just to give them a chance to eat. But if the throwing continues, be done.
- You shop, you serve the food. Parents worry so much about what their children eat. As the parent, you set the parameters of what your children eat. You shop and decide what food comes into the house. You put the food on the table. If you are fine with the food you serve, then you can back off the question of what they are eating. Young children tend to have smaller appetites than we think and it is always unpredictable as to what they will eat at any meal. The best way to

handle this: Put several items on their plate, and leave it to them to eat as they wish. Some may be picky and not like any foods to touch each other; respect that. But also put other foods out on the table for them to choose from—cheese, carrot sticks, olives. They can take what they want, in amounts they want; this will help them know how much they want to eat so they can begin to regulate their own food intake. And they love having control. Being able to take from the table platter gives them choice and control. At our center, we put trays of rice cake out on the table. Every child takes as much or as little as they want. They love it!

- Take them shopping. Take your child to the grocery store or farmer's market. Having him help you pick out the food (do you want cornflakes or Wheat Chex?) lets him be part of the process. They also see where food comes from—the store, the farmer's market—and they feel proud to do what the adults do.
- Don't be a short order cook. Parents can give children far too many choices. You, the parent, decide what to serve. If your child resists a certain food, but you've provided options that you know he eats, then he can decide on what to eat. Always serve at least one thing you know he likes (for my children that was always bread!). In other words, don't be the one policing what and how much a child eats once you put the food on the table.
- Avoid offering treats or making dessert contingent on eating dinner. Treats and dessert take on way too much importance and will hijack a toddler's attention and desire. Instead, treat all food

the same. Some of what they eat will be sweets or snacks. Make it part of their regular eating rather than a special treat. The "special" or "forbidden" foods will take on a life of their own and your child will beg, plead, or whine for them. It becomes the destination of a one-track mind. Avoid that by not making any food into something so special. Still battling? Don't have food in the house that causes such conflict.

We had a family at our center whose child begged and screamed for gummy bears every single morning. He was told no by mommy, and no by daddy, who said repeatedly, "We don't eat candy for breakfast." But every morning there were fits and screaming. They offered him many options, but all he wanted was gummy bears. The result? He came to school hungry, as he would not eat breakfast. We suggested they put a small bowl with gummy bears at his place when they served him breakfast. Crazy as the idea sounded to these parents, they tried. Sure enough, he ate breakfast, every morning. And after only one day, he did not even eat the gummy bears. He just wanted to be sure he had them. It's all about control!

- It is not about manners. Yet. It is all about you. Most of us prefer to be with polite children. I do. But don't expect proper manners at this age, from "please" and "thank you" to sitting up straight at the table or using utensils just right. Your child learns from you. If you treat them with respect, say please and thank you to them, and sit nicely at the table, they will learn to be polite as they get older.

How to Chat with Your Toddlers and Avoid Food Battles

As your children get older, dinner is a time when they will tell you about their day. Few children respond to direct questions (at any age) but most will chat as the meal goes on if there is no pressure on them. You can use these early ages as a time to set up routines and behaviors that will serve you well when they are older and have more to say. When mine were all elementary age we played a game at our table: "Who had something funny, bad, good, or strange happen today?" This gets people talking without being put on the spot. It also recognizes that in any day good and bad both occur. Often, my husband would start. It could be as simple as "I saw something surprising today. On my ride to work I spotted the first leaves changing color on a tree. Two yellow leaves. And it is only August!" This breaks the ice. Then the boys usually started sharing pieces of their day, sometimes arguing over who got to talk.

With the conversation running, leave it to your child to decide when he is done eating; this is how they learn to respond to their hunger and satiety signals. If your toddler is one who jumps up quickly, after a bite or two, simply say, "You know if you are full. Have you had enough to eat?" And remind her that the meal is finished! In time, they all learn to eat what they need, but only if we, the parents, don't keep interfering. The bottom line: Do not notice what your children eat. Simply serve, chat, and enjoy. I know it's easier said than done. But it makes for better family relationships all around.

How do you handle, later in the evening, "But I'm hungry!"? Maybe your child is going through a growing spurt. Or they did not eat much for dinner. Or they are simply testing their power. The best way to handle this is to take yourself out of the battle *before* it even begins. Give them part of their wish by making food available, but limited. Leave one food out on the counter in a bowl for them. "There is always cut apples; other fruit; carrot sticks. Help yourself." Doesn't sound appealing? One night my kids whined, "But we are tired of cut-up apples!" I lovingly reminded them to eat more dinner next time. Battle over.

• Getting Dressed •

Getting dressed is the first step toward starting the day, and from your toddler's point of view that often means saying good-bye. So yet again, this task involves all the feelings of separation. It is another place where choices come in to meet your child's need for control. So many children dawdle or are distracted by whatever they see or want in the moment rather than focusing on getting dressed, a task that could be done in mere minutes. Take a moment to consider the toddler mind-set: "I just woke up [even if it was two hours ago] and now I am with Mommy and Daddy again, after a long night's sleep. And now I have to prepare for a day and good-bye? No way."

They are far from being in a get-ready-for-the-day mode. You can see where the conflict comes in as you, the parent, have a goal toward starting the day. Our adult time pressures (to get to work, or get children to school or classes) clash head-on with the toddler's tried-and-true mode of living in the moment.

With this toddler frame in mind, the goal should be to help them become more independent in dressing *over time,* and to avoid battles. Keeping the longer goal in mind can help get through the day-to-day getting-dressed crises (although you may be lucky enough that this is not a place of conflict right now for you and your child). You guessed it: For some children, what to wear is a battleground for testing power and showing you who they are. You have ideas about what they will wear, but so do they. So kids ages two to five need varying degrees of choice when it comes to their clothes. Some children will wear anything, while some have very specific ideas (only one color; only one texture; long sleeves even in the summer). But for the most part, they need your help, especially at the younger ages—this means a couple of limited choices and assistance (and patience) to get dressed. Over time, they will do much more on their own.

What to Do

Like any other task that is done daily, routines create a daily structure that helps children grow more independent. And at times when your child really needs power, or to show you who she is, clothes are a way to do that; that's when you hear "I pick out what *I* want."

Here are some guidelines:

- Prepare in advance. The night before, put out two outfits so your child can choose in the morning what to wear. I always did this the night before, but some families find it easier in the morning. Either way, you are giving choices, but limited ones.
- Again, give limited choices. "Do you want this red shirt or the blue?" "Do you want a dress tomorrow or long pants?"
- Less is more. Keep fewer clothes in their drawer or closet so that they are not overwhelmed with possibilities; too many options will drive you both crazy and make it impossible for your child to settle on one outfit.

- Help them, but let them do what they can, especially for younger toddlers. You hold the sock, they push the foot in. You hold up the shirt, he puts his arm up and in. In no time you will have a three- or four-year-old who dresses herself and surprises you. And feels great about his accomplishment.
- Make it a game (humor required). Children can put up all kinds of stall tactics or hesitate to get dressed. Remember, they don't want to proceed to leaving or saying good-bye, even if fun lies ahead. They only know that at this moment, they have your attention (even if you are yelling). In this case, make dressing a game, and keep it light and fun. You cannot imagine how many times I've had socks and other odd clothing items on my hands or my head that my little one grabbed and instantly put on his feet, saying, "Mommy, that is not where they go!"

• Getting out the Door •

As many a parent will tell you, toddlers like to dawdle. They don't seem to listen to you when you give them a five-minute warning; they don't seem to remember how much fun they had yesterday when they went to preschool or the playground. They are stuck in the moment and find every way not to head toward the door. Battles, meltdowns (of toddlers and of parents!), and delays getting out in the morning are among the most common complaints from parents of children this age. Leaving home is not easy! At this point you probably know why. It is leaving the comfort of the place they know best, and because they live for right now, they can't really focus on where they will be after they leave home. Whether it means good-bye to daddy or mommy, or simply to home, getting out of the house can be a challenge. Once again, think about separation.

What to Do

Getting out the door is a big transition, no matter how much fun they will have on the other end. It is separating from home and often from you. As redundant as it may sound, morning rituals and routines are helpful; in fact, there really is no other way to smooth out this transition.

- Be organized ahead of time. For example, keep their coat, shoes, and sand bucket or other outdoor items in the same place so they can be part of the getting-ready routine. When they know where their belongings are, they get used to the routine faster and can handle more of it on their own, with reminders. When my children were younger, I had all their items lined up by the door the night before—backpack, shoes, socks and coat. In the morning after breakfast, I could give them reminders: now it's time for shoes; grab your coat; backpacks on. And they could follow through.
- Reminders as guidance. Children need reminders for each step (first your socks, now your shoes; get your coat), and in time (sometimes a long time or even years) they learn the sequence with fewer reminders, and later do it themselves (much later for most children). Some children are naturally better at it than others. Structures for organizational skills are

developing in the brain, and reminders are a necessity to move the development forward.

- Transitional objects are important. For many children, taking a toy or other object with them from home to school (the same thing every day, or a different object), or even to the park, helps to bridge the transition. I think of it like lucky charms that adults carry, or even the photo of your child you may keep in your wallet. You take a piece of what you know with you. Children often like to do this, too. There are the regular items—blankies, stuffed animals, a car, truck, or doll. But I also know children who leave with a toothbrush or random piece of Lego, a single puzzle piece, or dog's toy. Whatever they take is fine, whether it is the same thing each time or something different. It helps them move from the place they know best—home—out into the world.

Parenting POV
When Routines Are Broken

All routines are broken. Whether it's grandmother visiting, or the family going on a vacation, or someone getting sick (parent, child, or sibling), such changes necessarily break any routine. This is when all the other time you've spent helping your child stick to a bedtime, teeth brushing, getting out the door routine will come in very handy: you can calmly explain why today is different and return to the routine when the "disruption" is done. The routine is the base, "disruption" the exception. This is an opportunity for children to learn, over time, how to be flexible themselves.

Routines are part of daily life and help move the toddler into a similar, familiar flow, day in, day out. Routines provide an inherent structure and are the grounding that leads your child toward greater independence. Routines bring comfort because your child has an idea of how things will happen and can begin to expect what will come next. This is especially important because they lack any real sense of time. Unlike adults, who set their days around a clock, a toddler's natural flow is haphazard and chaotic, so they need predictable routines to guide them. Routines organize their day, and help them feel organized inside. These are all skills that set up your child for success in their daily life going forward. But they need our help, and at these ages that means sticking close to them with reminders and reassurances, and the flexibility to help through changes.

chapter six

Cracking the Code on Toddler Emotions

Tantrums, Fear, and the Battle of "No!"

One afternoon, a toddler in absolute hysterics could be heard screaming down the hallway, on his way to our center. He arrived shrieking, stomping, and mad. His mother, understandably, was exasperated. "It's enough," she said. "You can do it later, just stop this now." Over the child's escalating screams the mother told this story: "Every day when he comes to school, he wants to push the buttons for the elevator. If we are the only ones, not a problem, he can. But today there was someone else waiting by the elevator, and she pushed the up button. He got upset and I said he could push the button inside. But absentmindedly, when we got in, I pushed it without thinking. Whoa! You would have thought the worst thing in the world had just occurred. He got hysterical, screaming, 'No! I push it! I push it!' And would not stop screaming. I had to practically drag him out, and now he won't stop." She paused for a moment, looking at this angelic child in hysterics. She was quite upset herself and stated firmly, "He needs to learn that he cannot always have his way!"

What was going on here? From the mother's point of view, it was just a button. There would be other chances to push an elevator button and her son needed to learn that he couldn't always "get what he wanted." Reasonable? For an adult, yes. As a goal for your child over time—to learn to handle disappointment? Absolutely. But not in the moment when he had an established routine and was on his way to school, where he would have to say good-bye. From his two-and-a-half-year-old mind's view, he had a ritual, and he knew just what each step was. And someone had the nerve to push the button outside of the elevator, disrupting his ritual and comfort zone. He recovered (just barely) from that, and then the worst possible thing happened. His mother pushed the next button. What did this feel like to him? Anger. He was intruded upon. "How dare you push the button that I *need* to push before going to school! I know my ritual and you just *ruined* it!" As odd as it may sound, that is how it feels to the two-and-a-half-year-old.

What did we do? First, the teacher said to him, "You wanted to push that button so badly." He got a bit quieter, then screamed, "I WANTED TO PUSH IT!" And then we insisted that the mother walk back down the hall and let him push the button. The mother thought we were overdoing it. "Won't that just spoil him? He can't always have his way," she said.

"No," we insisted, "this is not spoiling," and explained why her son felt so enraged over having a plan that he could not carry out, and why it was important that she step in and remedy the situation with him. In time, he will learn to be flexible, but now he needs what he needs, especially since it is part of separating. Situations of frustration and anger cannot always be redone. But in this particular case, it could be. She walked down the hall and let him push the button outside of the elevator. He proudly sauntered back in, feeling validated in his needs and ready to be part of the toddler group.

• The Emotional Lives of Toddlers •

The emotional life of the toddler is intense. Just as her behavior swings from one extreme to another, her inner (and outer) emotional life is just as extreme. Toddlers are in the throes not only of learning to express their feelings but of learning to understand them. Their little brains are busily trying to figure out the world outside them and the world inside them . . . and many times, nothing seems to make sense. Of course, as you are probably guessing by now, toddler emotions play a large role in how they behave. From a brain perspective, their brains are on overdrive trying to regulate and process all the incoming information—and this processing is a highly emotional activity. It's no wonder that our toddlers are emotional creatures!

Three-year-old Tammy requested a piece of toast. As her mother was preparing it, Tammy sat at the table and chatted away. She eagerly awaited her toast and told her mom that she wanted to wear the new shoes to play outside later. The mother asked, "Do you want butter?" No. "Jelly?" Yes. Strawberry. She asked all the right questions, knowing that children this age are very particular about what they want to eat. The mom took the toast, spread the jelly, cut the toast in half, and served it to Tammy on her favorite plate. Instead of a smile of satisfaction for getting what she requested, the child was apoplectic: "Nooooo, no, no! I DON'T WANT IT. You cut it. I want a big piece. Only a big piece." And with that she shoved the plate nearly across the table, crying and upset.

What happened? First a sweet child, chatting about the day, and a mother responding to her request for toast, no butter, only jelly, and strawberry jelly, to be exact. Next, in the blink of any eye, there is an out-of-control child responding as if her world has just come to an end (which in her mind it had). In this case, the child had an idea in her head, of a big square piece of toast, smothered with strawberry jelly. A big piece, a whole piece, is important to children this age. (They desire it all—and all means whole. Cut means broken. Broken is frightening.) Her expectations are clear to her, so they must be clear to everyone else, she thinks. She lives in this very moment with ideas of her own. She sees the toast, and to her great dismay, it is cut. *HALVES? You've got to be kidding me! Now it is all broken! I* need *it whole.*

Toddlers have ideas, clear and particular ideas, at least to them. But they can get ambushed by their emotions of the moment, and when they are, breakdowns follow.

As always, parents and close caregivers often get caught in the toddler's emotional storm. Some of these storms are pleasant—when a child is filled with exuberance and joy, happy, delighted, surprised, or interested in you or something around them, there is nothing more engaging and uplifting, to the child and to you! It is these mutually satisfying and cooperative shared moments that provide building blocks for your relationship with your child.

However, it's when toddlers experience and then try to deal with more negative emotions that our interactions with them become tangled up. Emotional eruptions can happen fast (I am referring here to toddlers' emotional eruptions, but you may feel that such eruptions happen quickly for you, as a parent of a toddler, too). Just like us, toddlers feel sad, frustrated, angry, and frightened. Just like us, they have complicated reactions to these negative emotions. Their inexperience and young, still-developing brains make handling these emotions ever more challenging, for them and for us.

First they are flooded with negative emotions they do not yet have the ability to understand. In an instant, they react. Do I push the feeling away? Act on it in this moment? Is it all right to feel this way? Am I bad for feeling this? Should I hide or run out of the room? Should I laugh and laugh because this does not feel good and I don't know what else to do? Should I put my head down and be silent and hope no one sees me?

Toddler Mode

These are some of the responses toddlers may have. As a parent, keep in mind that toddlers lack the brain-based skills of thoughtful planning to think about these questions, weigh solutions, and then choose the best possible way to act. Instead, they act, quickly and in the moment. In contrast, adults will remark, in response to something they did and later regret, "I just wasn't thinking." Consider this the toddler mode. Not because toddlers are uncaring and thoughtless beings (although it appears that way at times) but because they are still developing the ability to stop, think through a situation or feeling, and then carefully select a response. Neuroscience studies validate that this is actually as it should be: the brain structures for carefully thinking through situations and planning responses are in development, but quite raw still. The same is true for the brain areas that regulate emotions so they don't overwhelm the child. Still raw.

Toddlers, as we've been seeing, are not really thinking about you or anyone else in the midst of an intense emotional response. They can't. They are completely absorbed in the feeling, in the intensity of the need that is driving or triggering the feeling, or even causing shame. For instance, when three-year-old Johnny realizes that he is missing the final piece to his puzzle, he bursts into tears. No amount of you telling him that it's okay is going to quiet him down. He is upset because he'd been working ten minutes (a very long time indeed) on this puzzle and he looks forward every day to the repeated satisfaction and the feelings of accomplishment of putting in the final starlike piece in the center. It's part of his daily routine. Where did it go? He is horrified, deeply frustrated, and so disappointed!

Johnny's disappointment and sense of loss are as real to him as if you had lost something dear and precious—a pet or a best friend. Loss is loss, and it triggers deep emotion. For parents, it's often difficult to keep the context of our toddlers' experience in mind. We don't think of the loss of the puzzle piccc as a big deal, or cutting a piece of toast in half as anything serious. Elmo is not on today? No big deal, it'll be on tomorrow. But for our toddlers, these events are devastating. Again, when we shift our point of view, and continue to see—and even feel—the world through our young child's eyes, then we may not be as quick to judge or shrug off their feelings. Seeing it their way gives us a different view that connects to their experience and brings them comfort so they can move on. For us as parents, this means less conflict and more harmony with our children.

Here is another example. Four-year-old Madison, seated at her kitchen table, was leaning back in her chair, pushing as hard as she could, so that the front legs of the chair lifted off the ground. She felt empowered and big—"look how strong I am." Glancing over from his position at the stove, her father quickly reacted, fearing she'd fall backward. "Madison!" he barked, "don't do that!" Instantly, the chair returned to position, Madison's head went down, shoulders hunched, and her breathing got heavy. "I just didn't want you to get hurt," her father calmly told her. "Madison? Are you upset? I was trying to help you not get hurt, honey." No response, head remaining down and body held tight. As he got closer to her, she swung her arm at him in anger. A parent's protective and instant response (surely preventing an accident in this case) can feel differently to the child. Madison was feeling strong and big, and suddenly she had a mixture of anger, sadness, and shame. Even with the best intentions, and to keep his child safe, the father's actions led to a negative response and the need for repair. That can be the required solution for parent and child: to repair a broken moment and come back together.

Clearly, all these parents had caring intentions and meant no harm. But if we understand the impact of our responses on our children, and if we understand why they may react as they do, then we are better equipped to help them learn about and manage their emotions, handle disappointment, tolerate negative feelings, and learn to experience them so they can move on. The alternative is for children to get stuck in these moments because they are so ashamed, or feel so badly, that they do not know how to move beyond this negative moment. If you cannot accept an emotion as being a part of you, then it is hard to let go of it. Children can become shut down with shame, or lash out in anger, stuck in the experience of the negative emotion. Negative emotions are confusing at this age (as they can be at most ages), and our toddlers need our help to handle them.

However, I do want to be clear about something: I am not suggesting giving in all the time, nor am I suggesting that you avoid negative emotions. What I highlight here is that our role as parents is to help children become better able to understand and navigate negative emotions, over time. Experiencing anger, fear, and disappointment is a natural part of being human and a big part of the toddler years. But so is facing limits—their own or those that adults set. Do you want a child who can handle life's setbacks, hurdles, and challenges? Do you want a child who can bounce back from the simple everyday stresses—when a friend won't play, when he doesn't get the seat he wanted at snack? Who can handle more complicated stressors at home without falling apart? One of the best ways parents can help toddlers build these lifelong skills is by helping young children navigate their negative emotions. In many ways, I see this as your number-one role.

So how does a parent do this? Let's take the examples above. For Johnny, whose expectations of completing the puzzle were shattered by a missing piece, even a little empathy can go a long way. By seeing the loss from his point of view, his parent can emphatize with him. "Oh, that is so frustrating. Where is that piece?! You really, really *need* that piece!" Empathy is what helps a child (and adult!) feel understood, which helps them settle down from the upset. At the same time, labeling their feelings is a necessary step toward helping them know over time what they are feeling. You could then try to look for the piece, or note that maybe you will find it later. Your recognizing his frustration and need for the piece helps him calm, regroup, and move forward. The arousal in the brain comes down (more on this below).

In the case of Madison, the issue is in the repair, the makeup after the fight. The father had to keep her safe, and reacted out of sudden fright on his part. But she doesn't know that. All she knows is that she was having fun and suddenly daddy yelled at her; she knows he got angry but she can't understand why. She is left confused and upset, coming to the conclusion that, *I must be bad for what I was doing. Daddy is so mad.*

Shame will flood her (see chapter 4 on the perils of shame). In situations like this where you overreact (even if you feel you had a right to be mad), go back and repair the situation by talking, in an age-appropriate way (clear, honest, and to the point; they don't need a lecture!) with your child. Children are frightened by a parent's anger no matter how justified the parent feels in having it. In the case of Madison, you might say, "I didn't mean to scare you like that; it's not your fault. I got so worried that you would get hurt, that I yelled. I'm sorry I yelled at you. I still love you, even though I yelled to stop." Your apology allows your child to see that the people she loves and counts on get angry, but they are still there for her. It rids her of blame and takes away any shame caused by the incident. At the same time, it puts her on the path to knowing that negative feelings happen in loving relationships, and there are ways to reconnect, which is an important model for helping her accept her own mistakes and learn to apologize and make up with others as she gets older. But, be sure you are ready for the repair. Insincere apologies, or one that is actually asking your child not to be mad at you, will leave a child confused and upset.

In both examples, the parental words and actions bring the parent and child back together. The repair and recognition of their experience help the child settle back down. And even if it takes your child a while to settle (some children's reactions are more intense emotionally and will need more time to subside), you have shown him you are there to provide help and comfort, even in rough times. How relieved he feels to know this!

When you see responses from the child's point of view, it helps you understand and label what they are feeling, which helps your child feel understood, and in turn brings down his emotional arousal, even if you can't change the situation or undo what happened. Again, it does not mean giving in to every demand or desire. It means seeing what they see, and connecting to their emotional reactions.

Here is an illustration of how recognizing their desire works. A mother was driving to visit out-of-town relatives. Her two-year-old was in the backseat and requested apple juice. There was none, only water. As many of us can understand, the mother became tense, fearing a crying match with another hour to go in the car. She responded empathically, "Oh, you want apple juice? We don't have it right now." An escalating cry for *AAAAPPLE JUICE!!* To which the mother said, "I know you want it, you love apple juice. We'll have it at Grandma's. For now, there is water." The mother kept her fingers crossed, hoping to avoid the tantrum. Her child fussed a bit, but quickly settled and reached for her sippy cup of water. Her desire was recognized even when it could not be satisfied. Remember that everyone—especially a toddler just getting to know herself—wants to be understood and recognized. A little bit of genuine empathy can go a long way.

You may be wondering why something so simple can be so effective. As I watch toddlers, I see how often we, the adults, don't really get what they are communicating, thinking, or desiring. So, in these instances of recognizing what they want or need (no matter how ridiculous that may seem from an adult point of view), they are overcome by a feeling of "Oh, Mommy [or Daddy]—you *do* get it. You *do* know what I want [or feel]." And this feeling of acceptance and being understood is very satisfying for all of us.

It is also important to remember that emotional responses can be quiet and internal, as well as outward and explosive. Parents and caregivers talk mostly about tantrums (for obvious reasons) but can overlook the quieter, inward, but still intense responses. A behavior we see in toddlers in our program involves standing back and quietly observing other children before trying something new, such as climbing up on a large climber. One day, a little boy, who had been watching from afar for many weeks, slowly approached the climber steps, and the teacher could see he was about to climb. An exuberant child ran over from across the room and excitedly pushed this little boy aside as she quickly and agilely scaled up the steps and slid down the slide, with great self-assuredness. Our cautious toddler stood silently and did not move from his position, just beside the climber. The teacher noted, "I know you want to go up the slide. Next time, you can say, No! There is always room for you, too." She put out her hand in a gesture that said he could still come forward. He quickly perked up and carefully climbed, taking his time. The recognition of his desire, ever so quiet, was important to help him move forward.

What to Do: Validate Their Feelings

A little empathy and recognition go a long way . . . and helps toddlers understand what they are feeling by labeling the emotion. Instead of simply directing them away from their feelings, take a moment to name it:

"I see how badly you wanted that toy. That is so, so frustrating!"

"That made you so mad."

"You seem to really miss Mommy."

"You really wanted to see Daddy tonight."

"I wish I could pick you up at school today; I know it makes you feel good."

"That scared you when the loud ambulance went by. It was really loud."

"I know it's so hard to wait. Mommies [daddies, teachers] are so slow, it is hard to wait for them!"

• What Are Emotions Anyway? •

Emotions drive all of our behaviors. How one feels will tell you much about what they can and will do. Emotions underlie how we think, how we communicate, how we respond to the world around us, and how we make decisions. Emotions are a large part of why we do what we do. For toddlers, who are just beginning to get their sea legs, these emotions are new, raw, exciting, and often very confusing! Recall from chapter 1 that the part of the brain that handles emotions and allows us to regulate them is just starting to form in the toddler, a process that will take another twenty years to complete. To say that handling these emotions for children ages two to five is hard is a major understatement.

As we've been discussing throughout the book, toddlers are driven by several core, elemental needs. And it is these core needs—the drive to separate, to figure out who they are, and at the same time the deep need to know they are not alone (meaning that you, the parent, is available for them)—that are intense and often clash. "I want you—I don't want you." "I want to do this myself—I want you to help me." "Leave me alone—Wait! Don't leave me." These clashes have an emotional base. I think of it like a barometer. Your child is playing and has a feeling of *I am okay on my own; I am content*, but then has a moment of *Where is Mommy?* This arousing thought motivates her to look for you. She looks over, sees mommy close by (*Phew! I am not totally alone*), and the barometer comes back down; the child returns to play. But if in that moment she does not see you, the barometer will shoot up (heightened arousal) and she becomes upset and fearful (*Where is my mommy?*). Now the behaviors follow: she may cry, come looking for you, scream for you, or behave in some other way to meet her need for knowing where you are. Now, combine these drives and the clashes with a brain that is a work in progress, and it equals raw emotions without the capacity to handle them yet, on her own. Hence we come to the intensity, the mercurial nature, the unpredictability, and the downright frustrating and irrational behaviors of a toddler. I assure you that your sweet little son or daughter intends no harm. They are just trying to figure out life.

In order to get their needs (which all have an emotional underpinning) met, toddlers try with their still-rudimentary ways to express themselves—sometimes in words, sometimes with their bodies, sometimes in their actions and behaviors. At times they successfully get across what they need; other times they are less than effectual. But before we get to how you as parents can best help your toddler move onto a path toward understanding and managing her emotional life, it might be helpful to take a step back and understand what emotions really are. During these years, you are their emotional bridge between the still-developing brains and limited experience in life, to the time when they can do more—and eventually most—of the emotion regulating for themselves.

Emotions have been a topic of discussion for thousands of years in fields as diverse as philosophy, medicine, psychology, biology, and animal behavior. Aristotle and Plato had theories. Darwin had theories. Emotions are a hot topic and a key part of what makes us human. A basic understanding of what they are, and how they work inside (and outside) us, will help guide your understanding of your toddler.

Emotion involves arousal and feelings and is tied to the central nervous system. At a basic level, emotions are triggered in response to something that happens in the environment, outside of the person, a stimulus. It can involve any of the senses, from seeing, to hearing, being touched, or tasting or smelling. When something occurs to or around a toddler, he or she reacts, in big ways or in small, sometimes unnoticeable ones. She might find the event stimulating in one way or another—either positive or negative. *Daddy's home? Hooray! My friend just touched my favorite stuffed bear? No way!* Or, she may not react at all, at least not outwardly (don't be fooled by what you cannot see going on inside, though). Children will automatically and immediately try to figure out if the stimulus that has occurred is good for them or bad for them, if they like it or not. For Johnny, the observation that the final prizelike puzzle piece was missing triggered an immediate, intuitive response: *This is terrible!* A different child, who had not been earnestly working on the same puzzle, in the same way and same order, for four days in a row, might have had a completely different reaction to the stimulus. Sophie could have observed a final piece was missing and simply walked away, either because she wasn't bothered or in resignation. Different emotional states, same behavioral response. Why children respond in the ways they do has to do with each child's inborn tendencies, experience, and relationship history. Ah—again, we see that no two children are ever alike! But understand that emotional arousal is the first response to an incident, which then combines with a child's individual characteristics and history.

Emotions often trigger (or are accompanied by) physiological reactions, another form of arousal. The flushed face of the excited child. The tears of the sad child. The rapid heartbeat of the scared child. The sweaty palms of the nervous child. The smile of the happy child. Just like us when we experience emotions, these body responses happen automatically during intense experiences of emotions and give us clues as to how children are feeling.

Emotions cause arousal—first internally, then externally. This is the barometer going up. Behavioral arousal is another aspect of emotion. Specifically, it refers to the body's response to the emotional situation. After a child assesses whether the situation is good or bad for her (often a quick and intuitive response at these ages), her body will react: it will become aroused in either a positive (engaged, interested, attentive, active), negative (feelings of stress, flight/fight), or neutral way (boredom, disinterest). When young children are working to manage their feelings, they are in part trying to calm down their arousal—to bring down their nervous systems, to return it to a state of less arousal. The barometer going back down.

A person's thinking and feeling are closely tied together and become a revolving cycle. Thinking and feeling go hand in hand in the brain, so which comes first is not easy to say. For example, when your three-year-old sees her grandma come in the door, she may feel happy. *I love Grandma, I am happy to see her.* She jumps up and down with a huge smile. But quickly another thought occurs: *When Grandma comes in the morning, Mommy goes to work,* and with that the child is flooded with sadness and anger and then, *Mommy! Don't go!* Tears and screams follow. Thinking and feeling fuel each other, and at this stage the flood of emotion makes it difficult for the child to manage the feelings. Her only recourse? A meltdown.

Recall how when our children are babies, we do the regulating for them. We pick them up when they are crying, we soothe them with hugs, kisses, close holds to the body. We sing to them, feed them, or rock them. We are trying to calm down their aroused nervous systems. And each time we calm them, it is a step toward them one day doing it for themselves. These interactions are encoded in the brain and help develop the emotional regulation structures. Toddlers are just beginning the long road of learning to handle this for themselves. But it takes time and will be punctuated with many fits and starts. And as you will see below, when they spend a lot of energy trying to manage intense arousal—positive or negative—their executive function (such as ability to focus or listen or to make a decision) is either enhanced or undermined. As you know, the hardest times are when it is undermined and your child falls apart in an emotional breakdown. At these moments the emotion arousal hijacks other parts of the brain, making it impossible for them to settle down.

But emotions are never just one thing: they are a "chain of events" that involves the environment, a child's appraisal of an event or situation (limited at these ages by their budding, but still new, verbal skills), the experience of the feeling associated with that appraisal, and then a behavioral or physiological response to that stimulus. This may sound too scientific an explanation; forgive me. I'm not asking that you dissect each of your child's emotional reactions. But keep in mind that their emotions are complex and dynamic interactions with the world, with themselves, and with you.

• Emotional Challenges •

As we've seen, the main tasks of children from ages two to five are managing the intensity of both needing you (the pull back) and the movement away (the push forward) so that they can become healthy, well-adjusted individuals. This process of separation comes in many shapes and sizes, often hiding in otherwise innocuous moments. Have you ever been in a room with your child, who is content playing on her own and you get up to use the bathroom just a few steps away? And soon you hear a howl and scream as if she is being tortured? She has been left by you. Abandoned, as far as she is concerned. This is her struggle—she wants to be on her own but is afraid of being left alone.

The child's ongoing struggle with the balancing act of being on her own (*I do it myself!* or even *Go away!*) and needing reassurance of your secure presence (*I just want to know you are there*) happens within a child's growing emotional development. At the same time that they begin to understand and express their feelings, they also are trying to manage them. Every piece of it is new. Toddlers are trying to express feelings, grab your attention so you can help them meet their needs, and learn how to monitor or resolve the feelings in a way that doesn't overwhelm or distract them completely. At the same time, you, the parent, are trying to move them toward more socially acceptable behaviors. It is a lot to handle at this age.

Let's take a look at how negative emotions can be disruptive and challenging, since your child is starting to understand these emotions while lacking the full capabilities to handle them. Knowing this will better equip you as you help your toddler begin to manage his intense emotional responses. And at this age, emotions are just that: intense!

Anger

Kids get angry. More specifically, *toddlers* get angry. Such intense anger may have blindsided you. Many parents are shocked to discover that their little bundles of spoiled love, their angelic, happy darlings, do get angry. How could they when life is good and their parents are trying to meet their every need? You may be surprised to know that they *should* get angry; it is important that they are allowed to. And, in fact, it is not your job to cater to their every need. Tantrums, screaming, whining, aggressive behavior, throwing, hitting, biting, are all examples of angry behavior that can be tied to attempts to separate and stake out one's own territory. Often the question I get goes something like "Do you think this anger is normal or is something wrong with my child? She gets burning red in the face, can hardly breathe, is out of her mind, totally out of control. That can't be normal, is it?" In fact, it can be. As your child moves out in the world and discovers what it means to be her own person, she develops her own ideas and desires (frequently in conflict with her parents' ideas and desires for her). She has her own will, and can be seen as "willful." The anger comes as she discovers that she cannot do everything she desires to do, cannot have everything she desires at that exact moment, is limited by her own abilities and the limits that adults set, for safety or otherwise. Anger is her protest against what feel like personal injustices. *I have a desire and you are denying me of it!* Or *I know what I want right now, I just can't achieve it on my own.* Or *I have so many feelings and I don't know what to do with them.* How frustrated she feels at times.

Three-year-old Lionel is finally tall enough to climb on the ledge and reach the water fountain at the playground by himself. He climbs up, pushes the button, and as he sips, he also puts his tongue on the spout. His mother gently reminds him, "remember the rule we follow: No licking the fountain. Keep your germs to yourself." He listens—and goes back and does it again. She removes him and again reminds him of the rule, which seems perfectly rational from her point of view. But for him, he is denied the pleasure of what he can finally do for himself. What does he do? Cry, pout, and protest when she does not let him drink from the fountain.

Four-year-old Zoe comes home from school to find her

younger brother playing with her trains, which she has not touched in months. Before even saying hello, she is yelling, "You *have* to ask me first. Mommy, you always let him play with *my* things. That is mine!" She storms down the hall and slams her bedroom door. After a long day at school, Zoe feels jealous and upset that her mother has been with the younger sibling all day.

The mother of two-year-old Lee has been away at a cousin's wedding. She returns after the weekend and brings Lee a gift she is sure will make her happy. Lee greets her mother with open arms, excited to see her. But within a few minutes she starts whining and tries to hit her mother. Yes, she is happy to see her, but now she is expressing the anger over her mother going away. Nothing the mother does pleases Lee, not even the present. Eventually, Lee falls to the floor in full meltdown mode.

Many parents think their role is to make children happy. Meet their needs and they will be happy. But think about it. Your child knows how to be happy. Give him a lollipop? Happy. Let her splash in a mud puddle? Happy. Play run and chase, over and over again? Happy. They don't need us to make them happy. And even if you wanted to make them happy all the time, it would not be possible (and not good for them; more on that later). In fact, the exact opposite is true. Your most critical role as parent is *to help your child through the negative* feelings, disappointments, and life's hurdles. Think about it this way: no one can be responsible for making another person happy all the time. But if you don't help your child learn how to manage frustrations, anger, and setbacks when they are young, do you think they can magically do it later? Now is the time, in your loving care, that you can help them learn to handle negative feelings, in themselves and others, and set them up for success in life, learning, and relationships.

Thinking about your main role as parent this way may

surprise you, at least initially. But when you view it from your child's side it starts to become more clear: your child has a right to his feelings, even when his reaction does not make sense to you. What does this mean? Don't try to simply squelch the bad or negative feelings. Instead, try to find out what's at the root of these feelings. It is easy for a young child to accept being happy. It is much harder to accept that they have bad feelings, too (*If I have bad thoughts and feelings, am I a bad kid? Do Daddy and Mommy still love me even if I get mad at them? Even if I wish they went away?*). Your role as parent is to help your child learn to handle these feelings and understand that even bad feelings are part of being a kid. It is a challenge for children, who are just beginning to understand who they are, to accept that sometimes they think, feel, and do good things, and at other times they think, feel, and do bad things. All of it is part of who we are, child or adult. If you help your child handle negative feelings, he or she is freed up to feel them, express them, accept them as part of life, and move on to happiness. It may sound simple, or even ironic, but the way to have a happy child is to help them handle the negative. Once you reflect back and label what your child seems to be feeling and why, he will learn gradually how to manage those feelings.

A couple came to see me about their four-and-a-half-year-old. The issue? Their daughter was "using a bad tone" when addressing her parents or asking for something. I hear this frequently from parents, and parents don't like it. Who would? It is like having a commander in the house bossing you around. It can be embarrassing, too. The couple reported that their child also whined often and threw tantrums when she did not get her way, or stormed away screaming, "I *hate you*!" Otherwise, they reported, she was kind and goodhearted, listened well in school, and had friends. I asked how they handled the bad tone and whining. They repeatedly told her that the way she was acting was "unacceptable and not nice." They had tried time-outs (which did not work) and found that the behaviors were increasing. They could not figure out why she would "act so rude." After all, they did not treat her this way, so where did she learn such behavior? I asked if she used this tone when she was angry. They thought for a moment, then agreed that was probably the case. They realized it mostly happened when a limit was set, such as "no TV or iPad right now." Perhaps this was her way of showing anger, I noted, and when they responded with punishment (time-outs) or criticism ("that is not nice"), it made her even angrier because she felt she was not being heard.

They were puzzled. I suggested that they shift their response. Rather than focusing on the tone and whining, they could instead label these moments as anger. "I understand you are really angry, that you don't like this; but I can't let you do that right now." This shift lets the parents connect to what the child's experience is while keeping a limit set. Within days, life was smoother and everyone was happier. They reported less whining, less angry tone, and their child (and parents!) moving on much faster from these confrontations. I am sure this four-and-a-half-year-old felt more understood.

• Tantrums •

Tantrums are a behavioral way of showing anger. Since children these ages have anger, especially as they come up against their own and outside limits, and are still learning how to understand these feelings, let alone manage them, you can be sure there will be tantrums. What else is a toddler to do at some moments? They lack the skills to talk you through their feelings calmly

(*Oh, Mommy, if you would kindly let me have one more piece of candy, then I will listen for the rest of the day, no need to worry*). Especially if they are already upset, they do not have enough control of themselves or their emotions to walk away, give a cold shoulder, or figure out a new plan; they can't even think through alternatives yet, due to still-burgeoning language and developing brain areas that help with planning and flexibility. Sometimes a tantrum is all they can do.

Tantrums are expressions of kids being completely overwhelmed by a situation or feeling inside them—frustration or anger—and lacking the words to express their needs. Remember the earlier discussions of executive functions and skills? Tantrums are the perfect storm—the intersection of brain development and the "separation/becoming me" process. In the midst of the child trying to separate and still hold on to a secure base (you), their brains are experiencing many new emotions before they have the structures or skills in place to handle them. Their regulation of emotions is still in development, at the brain level and at the skill level. So, no, your child is not intentionally trying to drive you crazy, but I know it can feel that way. I've been there. Rather, children these ages are working on their language skills, trying to name and understand their many feelings, learning how to manage these different and intense feelings, all while learning strategies for getting through them. Strategies like distraction or coming up with alternatives don't always work for them, but they will in time. Certain situations simply become too much. What happens at those times? Tantrums of many styles and sizes.

Jacob had just turned three and his parents felt relieved. He was talking more, loved trains, and would play for extended times on his own; he seemed to have fewer meltdowns, and life was getting easier. One day his father picked him up from school. Jacob ran to his father with open arms and a big smile, so glad to see him. They left school and he climbed into his stroller—all by himself! His pride was evident. He quietly sat in his stroller, tired out from playing at school, as his father said good-bye to the teacher and a friend. Jacob grew impatient, first asking for water, then for pretzels, then for candy. His father told him to wait and grew a bit impatient while parting with his friend. Next thing his father knew, Jacob flung his sippy cup right in the father's direction. His father got upset. "No! Jakey." From Jacob's point of view, he had been away from his dad and was happy to reunite; he was tired and ready to go, and had few resources left to wait. His father merely wanted two more minutes, but that was more than Jacob could bear. Now his father had yelled at him and Jacob began to scream. It escalated until he was thrashing, screaming, and banging his head back against the stroller seat. He was inconsolable. You can imagine his father's embarrassment, in front of teachers and other parents. You can also probably feel Jacob's frustration and need to leave, too.

The most important message I can give you in these moments is *stay calm*, this too shall pass. They won't tantrum forever (although it may be for longer than you'd like!). I say this after years of experience watching toddler tantrums and handling many in my own family. A child having a tantrum does not get better when the adult tantrums, too! At the point of the tantrum, your child has told you she is overwhelmed and over the edge. She cannot listen or be rational in the midst of it. Don't make demands of your child, don't try to cajole or negotiate, as she is too upset. Once they have hit the meltdown point, the best you can do is let them have the tantrum, and never laugh or shame them for it. This level of anger is actually frightening to them, too. They are literally beyond control themselves, their brains are overwhelmed, and they count on you to keep them safe. For some children, that means you sitting close by and waiting. Other children want or need to be held (some thrash a lot, so protect yourself).

These outbursts of anger often come at a point when you, the parent, are also feeling over the edge a bit. My best advice is to use all your well-developed brain skills (the ones your toddler has not yet acquired) to stay calm, not engage in the battle, and know that they won't tantrum forever. At the same time, this doesn't mean leaving your child—either by walking away or threatening to leave him (even when you feel ready to!). In the midst of their overwhelming anger, the idea of being abandoned is terrifying (and that is what it feels like if you leave the room). They will get scared thinking that they have the power to actually push you away. You may have experienced this: Your toddler screams, "Go away!" or "I hate you!" and you walk away. They frantically come running after you, even more hysterical. As angry as they are, they really need you. That is the battle of needing to be separate and needing to know they are not alone, all at the same time. Life can be hard at two, three, four, or even five.

• Handling Your Own Anger and Upset •

Sometimes as a parent, we can also get embroiled in the battle and become just as upset as our child. We want to explode. It is all understandable, especially if your child feels challenging on a day-to-day basis, or if your generally mild-mannered three-year-old erupts in meltdowns out of the blue. The problem is this: our young children need us to stay calm, reasonable, and in the adult role. Want your child to grow into a reasonable person over time? They learn it from us! So what can you do? Find ways to bring yourself down. For many years, I had a mantra that I used in my head. I'd take a deep breath, maybe a step back (without leaving the room), and say to myself, *He's just a little boy. He's just a little boy.* I'd repeat this inside over and over both to calm myself so I could help my child, and to see him as the struggling child he was in that moment. It is easy to forget how little they are, and how much they need us to be close and calm.

There may be times when you can see your child's anger starting to build before it has reached that point-of-no-return meltdown. In this case, try another strategy. You can help your child learn to label her own feelings, which is an important step in the process of learning to *handle* them, too: "You are so upset and mad that [he took your toy; you can't have cookies; etc.]." "You really wanted Sam to come over and play today. That is disappointing!" Match their tone, so your response meets the emotion they are experiencing. It conveys that you get what they are experiencing. Being insincere in your response will not help, just as it would not if a friend or your spouse acted insincere in their empathy to your upset. Labeling gives your child a sense of being understood while at the same time it helps them understand what they are feeling. Remember the barometer analogy. Empathy addresses a barometer that has gone up and brings it back to baseline.

A mother told me a story about her five-year-old. At a weekend-long family event, his younger sister was enamored by two older cousins. She spent most of the day with them, and ignored her brother. He kept telling the mother how mean these cousins were and how much he disliked them. He complained about many things that day. At dinner, when he could not sit where he wanted, he threw a fit (which was unlike him). This mother could not believe his behavior at age five, and began to think that maybe the cousins really were being that mean—until she realized what was going on. After dinner, she walked with him on the beach. "I bet that made you mad that your sister spent so much time with the big cousins," she said to him. "She didn't really want to be with you, like she does at home. That would've made me mad if I were you." He smiled in agreement and quickly perked up. The mother had labeled his jealousy. Even at five, when tantrums are fewer, your child still needs help understanding his negative feelings.

Children at this age don't yet know how they feel in these moments of upset. Labeling the emotion—"That made you so sad." "You were angry when he yelled no!"—helps them understand these tough emotions over time. Don't ever shame your child for what she is feeling. As a parent, it can be frustrating to watch your child throw herself on the floor because you just ran out of her favorite cereal. And when she throws her spoon across the room to show the anger, this seems even more bizarre (and infuriating). But when you shift your perspective even a little, her response makes more sense. In your child's head her most delicious cereal was about to be poured. And suddenly—bam!—that cereal was not available. She doesn't have the ability right now, this early in the day at age three, to handle it. So she cries, and throws. Negative feelings are part of being a child, even if a behavior needs a limit. "I know you wanted that cereal. I understand you're angry, but I won't let you throw. You can stomp your feet and yell, 'I'm mad!'" Saying this validates how your child feels but also helps redirect the anger to a more socially acceptable and less harmful behavior.

But sometimes as a parent, you feel stuck. You are out in public. Your child melts down. You brace yourself for the stares. The looks. The criticisms. What are you to do?! I recall being on a very open promenade in California when my then-two-year-old threw a huge tantrum. He was sprawled on the ground, unmovable and inconsolable, kicking and shrieking. All I could do was let him do it; I had failed at all attempts to ward it off. A man was approaching us on the walk, and I braced myself for some embarrassment or criticism from him about how bad my child was (or what a terrible parent I was). Instead, as this stranger got closer, he smiled and said, "This will pass. Mine were like this once and now they are adults. Enjoy these years all you can." I was so relieved. And I remind you of the same: This too shall pass. They are small people trying to figure out the world. And sometimes, that is a tall order for them!

If you are out of the house, try to move your child to a less busy place to help her calm down, regain composure, and feel safe. This is not punishment; rather, it is helping her manage the difficult emotions and accompanying behaviors. It may be hard to believe, but children don't like feeling so out of control. It is scary. The most important part of the tantrum is the repair that follows. When your child has settled down, make sure to come back together and let her know you are still here for her—with a hug, a loving coming together. "You were so angry. I am here and I always love you. Even when you are screaming and upset." It doesn't feel good to have a screaming child, especially in a public place. It can be quite embarrassing. But the bottom line is, your child needs to know you are there for them. No matter what feelings get expressed.

Negative feelings pop up or even erupt throughout a day, throughout our lives. Experiencing a range of emotions, from positive to negative, from mild to extreme, is part of what makes us human. For toddlers, these are new experiences and ones they don't yet know how to handle. Such emotions emerge out of their desire to be separate but secure, to explore but hold on to the familiar. As they come up against limits and

Parenting POV
Handling Anger

If we cannot accept our own anger, bad thoughts, or negative feelings, then it is much harder to accept that our children experience these same thoughts and feelings, too. Were you supposed to be the good child when you were growing up? Were you told that there was nothing to get upset about? Were you shamed for feeling badly? These experiences are in all of us and affect how we parent. Your child's most intense feelings will be directed at you (not at the babysitter or the schoolteacher). Why? Because children will show their true colors only to the one(s) they trust the very most—mommy or daddy. So be easy on yourself, and try to understand that it's human to have negative and intense feelings; every child has them, every adult has them. That way, when your child expresses "I hate you!" you will be less likely to take it to heart, knowing that the feeling is fleeting, and the words actually mean "I am so angry right now!"

boundaries—there to help them develop and keep them safe as they battle their own still limited skills—emotional arousal is set off. With their brains developing rapidly, but not fast enough to set up the structures yet to fully help them manage all of these emotions, there are meltdowns and tantrums in response to frustration, anger, and disappointment. These are all natural bumps along the way to mastering the self-regulatory skills that are so important as they move through toddlerhood and into the elementary, middle school, and adolescent years. In fact, each time they get through a tantrum, and you are there for support, and they see that life is back to being okay, it helps set into place these important regulatory skills.

Your role as a parent is to stick by their side and actively help them learn to manage these negative emotions so they can master self-regulation. Each time you model ways to cope and scaffold them as they struggle to stay on track (through routines, for instance), they will get a bit closer to being able to manage negative feelings on their own. But it takes time—a long time! Knowing how to handle the negative leads to happiness, persistence, and the ability to handle life's challenges. This can be seen clearly when we try to help our toddlers manage transitions, those that occur daily and bigger, one-time transitions as well. In doing so, you will set your child on the road to handling these hurdles throughout life.

chapter seven

Cracking the Code on Transitions

Helping Toddlers Manage Change

Three-year-old Annabelle is preparing a delicious Play-Doh meal she has carefully created, plates laid out on the floor all in a row, cups at each place, with bright red Play-Doh for the meal. She is busy crafting Play-Doh pancakes, cupcakes, and hot dogs. It's a lot of work!

Her mother calls to her loudly, "Time to get ready for school!"

As if not even hearing her mother, who is close by, Annabelle continues to prepare the fine meal.

"Annabelle!" the mom calls again. Annabelle continues her very focused playing.

Her mother comes into the room, now less upbeat. "C'mon, Annabelle, I said it's time to get ready. Go get your shoes on."

Annabelle quickly gets upset and cries, "No! I am playing. Lunch is not done!"

"But you love school. You'll see your friends," her mother reassures her.

Annabelle doesn't budge and the crying gets louder. Her mother sighs, thinking, *It is always like this when we have to go to school.*

Transitions are part of life, in big and small ways, daily or seasonally, or one-time happenings. A transition can be as innocuous as getting out of the tub and into pajamas and as dramatic as leaving the comfort of home and going to school for the very first time (or even the thirtieth time!). Transitions are physical—as in leaving one place to go to another. Transitions are emotional—leaving a comfortable and known place and adjusting to one that feels new or different, with all the worries, wonders, and fears that entails. Transitions are in the imagination—leaving the known for the unknown. Transitions can embody daily activities—lunch to nap. They can involve growing up moments—crib to bed. Transitions also mean life shifts—becoming a big sibling. Transitions can involve encountering new or strange environments or people. And for toddlers, anything that feels new or different feels scary even when it also feels exciting. They lose the comfort and grounding of the here and now and what they know.

Regardless of the size or frequency of transitions, transitions mean *change.* A transition is a move from the familiar-and-known (whatever I am doing now) to the new-or-unknown (even if I have done it before, it is new for this moment). Every transition involves ending the now whether you want to or not, and shifting focus to a beginning of something else. I think of the space between the ending and the new beginning as the great divide, the threshold that has to be crossed. That divide is the transition—one foot still in the old and trying to end, the other foot moving into the new. Sounds unstable? It is. The foundation gets wobbly and uncertain at times of change. And that is exactly the problem for the young child. None of us likes change, really. For the young child it is particularly problematic—they are all about sameness and transitions counter that head on. Think of a transition as a good-bye, a leaving behind of something—whether that is your pajamas when getting dressed or a favorite activity when it is dinnertime—or a hello and coming together with something on the other side—putting on clothes for the day, sitting at the table instead of playing. Transitions are change and require adaptation. Adaptation requires managing emotions.

The key to understanding how to help our little people to move through and manage any change of circumstances is again to think of the world from their point of view: they are stuck and bound to the present. Like us, they don't revel in change—it feels like being pulled in an opposite direction. Just as they are seeking independence, transitions force them to move on to something else, not usually by their own choice. And probably most important, they are not entirely secure in themselves yet. They still need us, precisely because they are not ready for full independence. And transitions tend to remind toddlers of this tightrope they are on.

What does this boil down to? Transitions are very charged for this age group. Lacking a sense of time, young children also lack a sense of sequence. They can't plan for what comes next. Living in the moment means that what they are doing right now is all they can think of, which is why moving on to the next thing is often difficult.

So it is no surprise that toddlers find transitions a challenge, and by default, parents do, too! The child who reads the same book every night before bed—twice!—and who insists on the same colored cup every morning for juice, who lines up her stuffed animals in the exact same order each morning at wake up, is not going to welcome change. Indeed, transitions stir up emotions: frustration and anger, confusion, anxiety, fear. It is these emotions that spark the challenging behaviors associated with transitions (tantrums, stubborn refusals, going limp, not hearing).

So how do we help our toddlers manage these tumultuous turning points? At the heart of any transition is helping a child switch his or her attention, to give up something currently known and focus on something else or new.

Let's go back to Annabelle. Does she really love school? And if so, then what is the protest about when her mother says to get ready for it? She does enjoy school and her friends. But there is a lot that has to happen for her to move from the current (playing at home) across that great divide to the next step (getting ready for school). Without framing her day based on a clock, suddenly she must shift her attention from the joyous Play-Doh meal she is preparing into a "going to school" mode. This involves stopping her play and letting go of what her attention is focused on. Then her focus must switch to something new—getting ready for school. Next she has to engage in this new activity—getting her shoes, her backpack. All in the midst of an emotional moment, for she knows she will be saying good-bye for the day. That is a lot to think about and a lot for the brain to do! Planning, flexibility, management, and organization are required.

Remember the discussions of brain development and executive function in chapter 2? These self-regulatory skills that help people through change are not well set for toddlers. That includes the flexibility to shift attention, plan next steps, manage emotions, and sequence (first socks, then shoes, then backpack). No wonder transitions cause so many problems. That is another reason why it's so important that we adults help toddlers with their transitions. If we think of these turning points as moments or opportunities for practice—when toddlers are trying on the habit of being independent—we can guide them more easily without as much hassle and fuss, for both parents and their kids.

Take Bryce, who at two and a half does not like transition times at school. They upset him. He cries when the toys are put away, or throws anything he can grab when the group gathers to go outside. But when Bryce eventually figures out that snack time always follows cleanup, he runs to the snack table on his own. No tears. He is the first to sit down and smiles proudly that he can do it himself. He feels in control and that is calming. After he has repeated the routine for going outside enough times over several weeks, he understands that gathering in the circle always leads to going outside, and the teachers stay with them. He is calmer. He eagerly gathers with the children and no longer throws. Mastering change is a major part of growing up. It takes a lot of repeated practice.

Everyday transitions help children become more flexible. But it takes time. For some children, more adult guidance and reminders are needed, and it can take longer to master. Flexibility is what allows children to handle the unpredictable nature of life—their best friend not at school today, the puzzle piece missing, a favorite shirt is too dirty to wear, it's raining so plans have been changed. A combination of experience, adult guidance, and brain development helps them become more independent in negotiating transitions. And the ordinary, daily transitions set them up to deal with the bigger life transitions—new baby, moving, going to a new school, loss. Day-to-day transitions are small stressors that provide practice and strengthen them to handle life's bigger ones.

Transitions from A to Z

We may not realize how many transitions a child has to handle. Here are some regular transitions that occur in children's lives—sometimes on a daily basis, sometimes in a more special or extreme time:

- Waking up, from sleep to awake
- Getting dressed, from pajamas to clothes
- Stopping playing to come to a meal
- Leaving home for school
- Breaking the routine of the week on weekends
- Turning off iPad or TV to move to another activity
- Going to bed for a nap or at night
- Giving up bottles or pacifier
- Going from diapers to underwear
- Coming home from school
- Saying good-bye to mom or dad when they leave for work
- Starting a new school or new class at school
- Moving to a new home
- Arrival of a new sibling in the family
- A visit for the week from grandparents or favorite relative
- A new babysitter
- Mommy or daddy coming home at the end of the day
- Vacations
- Getting a new pet
- The death of someone connected to the child

• Transitions: Getting from Here to There •

Think about all the transitions children face each day—asleep to awake, playing to the breakfast table, the breakfast table to getting dressed, playing on the floor to out the door into a car or stroller, home to school or home to playground, school back to home, out of the bath and mom's kiss good night to bed on their own. There are less frequent but larger transitions—a move from crib to bed, diapers to underwear, sleeping without the pacifier; a change or break in the daily routine; the birth of a new sibling; going to a new school; end of school to the summer. Many moments that may seem innocuous or exciting to us can be experienced by this age group as very challenging, confusing, frightening, or overwhelming.

Transitions are about leaving the comfort and safe feelings of the known, whether the known is home or this moment. If Jimmy is putting together his Lego house right now and daddy asks him to put away his toys and come eat lunch, he is going to feel put upon by that request—like that request makes no sense at all! Leave his toys for food? *What? You say lunchtime? But wait! I am not done playing.* Now it is unsteady ground. A lot of switching modes, attention, feelings, and actions has to take place.

Parenting POV
Transitions Are Hard

Most of us don't like change, and transitions are change. Think of the Sunday night blues as we leave the calm, relaxed comfort of the weekend to the beginning of the workweek. Or the return from vacation back to regular life.

When I left my apartment in labor with my first child to go to the hospital, I hesitated at the door before leaving. I looked back into the apartment thinking, *Something big is about to change. I don't know what it will be like when I return, but it will be different.* I didn't know how, I just knew an enormous change was about to occur. It is that excitement, trepidation, and fear all wrapped in one that transitions embody.

Rites of passage throughout life are transitions. Graduations are ceremonies that mark the completion and end of a specific level of education and moving on to the next, or out to the work world. They are times of celebration and of nervousness. I watch my college students approach their graduation with excitement, dreams, and fears as they embark on their next steps. Think about your own transitions and it can help you understand why even seemingly harmless ones are trying to your child. Recall a job promotion that you had been hoping to get. You were likely honored and thrilled to receive it but unsure of the new responsibilities and expectations you faced. Transitions raise a range of feelings, both positive and negative.

For children, even small transitions can bring up big emotions. As parents, we need to remind ourselves that some of these transitions are also sad for us. We think we celebrate all of our children's accomplishments on their road to maturity. But at the same time, we can acknowledge our own mixed feelings about our babies growing up. Even when we are happy about the change, we may feel stress or even anxiety around our own transitions as well as those our toddlers are experiencing. Happiness to have them out of a crib could also mean sadness at missing that little baby. You may be waiting and waiting for the diapers to come off, yet when they do, you can miss the baby who wore them. Happy to send them off to school, the one you carefully selected, sad that they are growing up. This is why there are so many tears at kindergarten graduations.

Every step forward for our children, all the ones we celebrate, also means letting go of the baby. Bed, bottles, pacifiers, schools, their own ideas, riding a bike, losing a tooth, are all developmental steps forward. There are two sides to all transitions. We need to recognize any feelings we have about missing the more dependent baby of yesterday. "I get so sad when she doesn't need me as much," one mother said after her child stopped crying at separation. Recognize the sadness of losing the little-baby side, even as you relish the growing up. It will help you enjoy your child's achievements and also remind you that they are still so little.

• Why Toddlers Have Trouble with Transitions •

Let's take a close look at why transitions are so thorny for toddlers. As you may recall, during this period of children's lives tremendous growth is going on in all ways—emotionally, physically, socially, and intellectually. One thing toddlers are struggling to achieve at this time is a sense of agency. Agency is that feeling that comes when children feel they have some control and can make an impact on their surroundings, to make the outcomes they desire happen. It is a great feeling to be able to make choices of their own (I can choose what I want) and having agency feels powerful. It can be as simple as pounding a hammer on a peg and seeing it go to the other side of the wood bench—"I did that!" Or struggling with a train track until the two pieces fit together. Agency is a positive outcome of becoming independent. The child feels they can handle themselves, can make choices and take chances. And this is a central piece of learning, feeling sure enough to try things because the child feels she can make something happen.

But when life feels out of their control, that they don't have an impact, it can be upsetting or scary. And that is what transitions feel like: moments that are thrust upon them. For toddlers, the unknown and feeling out of control cuts to their core and lays bare a strong vulnerability. And when they feel vulnerable, they react. They may get aggressive and angry, or quiet and sullen. We need to think of transitions as adjustments they are having trouble making, a time when they do not feel in control. During transitions, they lack the agency and sense of independence they are working so hard to acquire. They need our support in recognizing and getting through transitions. The story of Tyler shows how this process can unfold.

Tyler was born in New York to parents who were from Colombia. The only home he knew was New York. But when he was four, they moved back to Colombia. They prepared him for saying good-bye to his home, school, friends, and neighborhood. They made a photo book together and had a good-bye party. He was excited to go see his cousins and grandparents in Colombia. At first it was a honeymoon. He loved his new home and neighborhood, especially with his grandparents close by. He had a backyard and new friends. He loved his new bed. He looked forward to starting a new school. It was summer when they arrived, and school was out, but he asked to visit the school. His mother took him to visit, but there were no children yet, so all Tyler visited were the building and playground. He ran around, and his mom thought he looked very happy.

The only hint she had that all was not as it appeared was a passing comment by Tyler: "I want my old school back." At times, he asked when he could go back to his old school. Yet he still spoke excitedly about starting the new school.

A few weeks later, Tyler and his family went to an orientation party at the school. Again Tyler had a great time, played with new kids, and seemed at ease in his new environment. He was excited for the new school. His mother was relieved.

The very next day, however, he woke up early and announced to his mother, "I don't like this school! I want my old school back! Where are my friends?!"

What had been excitement was now upset. Tyler had handled many transitions in the move to a new country and home. A new school was just too much and the reality of his old friends not being there had sunk in. Soon the first day of school arrived. Tyler was apprehensive and quickly started crying when it was time to leave home. Again he said, "I don't like this school."

Despite the familiarity of his surroundings and family and relatives who knew and loved him, Tyler was still adjusting. His mother felt settled in after three months, but he did not. Any move to a new school is a big change. When he was first told about a new school in Colombia, Tyler likely pictured his old school, old friends, and old teachers. That was what he knew. That is the picture he would know. But upon actually seeing the school, the children, classroom, and teachers, he suddenly realized, *Wait! This is not my old school! This does not feel familiar! Where did everyone and everything go?!* He was upset!

So no matter how nice the parents tried to bill it, he felt unsettled with the newness. They knew it was a good school and they figured he'd adjust over time. But for him at age four, it was a different story. This was a huge transition, and with transitions come loss of whatever came before—whether it was two minutes ago, or in a bigger transition like a move.

His mother scheduled an appointment and called me quite upset, wondering what to do. "When he is home in Colombia, he sits for long periods and looks out the window. He stares out at buildings in the distance and calmly and dreamily says, 'I see Manhattan. See my babysitter? She is over there. I can see my real school.' "

When his mom shared this with me, it was clear to me what was happening. I explained that Tyler missed his old home, he had to grieve the loss, the good-bye. Transitions are a process and she could help him handle the feelings of loss and sadness that go with it. Then he could be happier about where he is. But the loss had to be recognized.

She began to talk to him about missing his old home and school and friends. He listened and began to ask questions. Sometimes he cried and pleaded to go back to his old school. As he tried to make sense of his new home, he began to ask questions: "Is the sky here the same sky we had in Manhattan? Do we have the same sky? Is it the same moon that we used to have?" He was trying to figure out his place and where he was in the midst of a big change.

He also needed to know that his old city and home still existed, that it was just far away. That is hard for children this age to comprehend.

Every year when our toddler program ends, we have to remind the children that the school will still be here; it is just closed for the summer, even when they go to a new school. When they come to visit in the fall or winter, they are truly relieved to see that it still exists. Tyler was expressing this same kind of loss and confusion.

Each day he started to settle a little more into school. Then one day he asked his mother if they could visit New York again. She assured him they would. He wanted to go immediately, today, right now. (He cannot understand the distance.) Her insistence that they could not go right away made him mad: "It is not far away! I can wake up there." She realized something that she had not thought about. When they left New York to move to Colombia, it was at night. Tyler was in his pj's. They got on the plane, he snuggled in and went to sleep. When he woke up, they were landing. From his point of view, the distance from New York to Colombia was not far. Imagine all of his confusion with this huge transition.

At four years old, Tyler cannot fill in the blanks of his situation the way we do as adults. He counts on the adults to provide him with a cohesive narrative about where he used to live and where he lives now so that he can understand more about what happened to him. This narrative provides stability and comfort through the transition and helps regulate the emotions the child feels. This is true whether the move is to a new school or new home or is about giving up bottles. For Tyler, the narrative is a story about how he got there—on a long, long plane ride, arriving at night. About the good-bye to New York and the new home in a new country. Tyler also needs to be told (likely again and again!) why they moved to Colombia; otherwise he feels like he did something wrong and this is punishment: "We moved because Daddy has a new job" and "Our family is here." It's also important to articulate to Tyler that his new home is far away, but New York is *still* there—it didn't disappear just because Tyler no longer lives there. His old school and friends are still there, and it is not his fault his family had to move to a new place. All of this is very confusing to a child. By telling the story that fills in the holes for him, and letting him know that there is a reason they moved and that this is not his fault, it frees him of the worry that he was bad and must be responsible for this change.

Perhaps the most crucial advice for Tyler's mother was to allow him to feel the sadness and anger of what he missed in order for him to move on. As we discussed in the last chapter, these negative emotions are important for children—they need to understand that it's okay to feel sadness, anger, longing. They need our permission and our support. I often hear this when parents move, especially a move out of their hometown to somewhere far away. Parents want to emphasize all the positives (and there can be many) but that overlooks the child's sadness, anger, and worry about moving and what they miss. And I suspect parents have these mixed feelings, too.

What to Do: Managing Transitions from Small to Big

Transitions mean giving up comfort. Transitions require adjustments. Even when the transition is good or exciting (a new dog, a birthday party), it is still new. Even if your child does something every day, what comes next is a change from what your child is doing right now. Any change to the current state of affairs is fraught with excitement and worry wrapped into one. Think of the daily transitions, the moments that move your child through most days (getting dressed, meals, leaving home, bedtime) as mini-moments of separation. Each one is a good-bye or separation from what they are doing. Bathtime is good-bye to play time. Breakfast is good-bye to snuggling with daddy. School is good-bye to home.

This is where routines come in. Routines put us on a necessary autopilot because the routine itself is comforting and familiar. They help your child feel in control and know what to expect. The circumstances may change, but the routine is steady. The child who dawdles each morning is showing her ambivalence about leaving the house. A common complaint from parents is the difficulty their child has getting dressed in the morning, even if it is an hour before leaving for school.

"She has not even had breakfast, we have another hour at home, but if I ask her to get dressed or even take out her clothes, she falls apart," one mother reported.

From the child's point of view, getting dressed means the start of separation. It may be an hour away, but dressed means they will eventually leave. Anything that gets them closer to good-bye is a transition at this age. It's hard for her to leave the comfort of home and mommy for wherever she is going. She may love school once she gets there, but that doesn't override her discomfort in leaving. She may dawdle over breakfast or finding her shoes. She may resist turning off the TV. She may need that extra one, two, or three hugs as she leaves you to enter the classroom.

Anything you do every day—from getting dressed to brushing teeth, to leaving home to eating meals—will be smoother if you have a routine to carry them through the transition. Many preschools sing songs at cleanup time. Why? Because that is their ritual—they sing this song and children know that means cleanup. At our school, as the toys are put away, the children run to the snack table. They might still want to play, but the routine ushers them over to snack. They have learned from repetition and practice that when the toys are put away, it is snack time.

• Moving to a New House •

Moving to a new home is a big change for toddlers. While you may be excited and know why you are going and where, your child does not. Some children handle these changes better than others, but for all children it is a major transition. For toddlers it means leaving the only home they've known. That can feel like a shock to the system. Home is comfort and security. Don't plan to make other big changes (giving up bottles or crib, toilet training) during a move to a new home, even if it is only around the corner. Children do best with one change at a time.

What Can You Do to Prepare Them?

Close to the moving date, but not too far in advance, explain to them that you will be moving to a new house. Their lack of time sense means you shouldn't tell them far ahead of time. It causes unnecessary anxiety for your child. Have conversations with other adults about moving away from their presence prior to this time. When telling them about the move, the most important piece to emphasize is that mommy, daddy, siblings—the whole family (and pets!)—will be together. Explain that all their toys, their books, their bed, everything will come to the new home. Children worry about what will happen to their possessions and need reassurance that the move includes all these items. Describe the new place and tell them about their new bedroom. If your child is old enough, he can pick out something for his room—new sheets, a pillow, a room color.

If you can, take them to see the new neighborhood and point out the house. Go to a local park or shopping area to help acquaint them. But remember that every transition includes a loss, and children need help with that part. They are giving up home, which is the known and familiar. To help handle this change, make a good-bye book of their current home with photos of their room, the house or apartment, and places in the neighborhood that have meaning to them (favorite playground, doormen, local grocery store). Include your child in the moving process so they feel part of it. On moving day (or a day before), let them have one moving box to put toys in. This way she feels assured the toys are coming. Also give her a backpack to put her most special items in (let her choose; you'd be surprised what goes in there!). Then she can carry the backpack and feel assured that she has her special belongings.

Parents are naturally inclined to talk up the good parts of a move, hoping their child will love it. I think it is a way to convince themselves of the move as well. But it is equally important to recognize what is missed, the loss.

A couple contacted me after they moved out of state. They felt guilty about pulling their five-year-old daughter out of her school mid-year for the sudden move due to a job change. So they planned a trip to Disneyland first, before settling into the new home. "We thought that way she would be happy. She would equate Disneyland with the new home." She loved Disneyland but she did not love her new home. She was angry at her parents, and they could do no right. She cried about missing school. She complained about the (much-improved) weather. She fretted the grocery store was "not like our real one at our old house!"

I pointed out to the parents that she was missing her old home and life. I asked how they were feeling three months into the move. They both admitted how much they missed their friends, old house, and neighborhood. Soon after, they visited their former city and friends. They took their daughter to visit her former school. There she told her friends about her new house, her new school, and how cool the garden at her new school was. She was excited to see everyone and proud to share her new experiences. Coming back, she was much more settled. And so were the parents. We have to mourn, and let our children mourn, the loss of the old so we can connect to the new place. Sadness and loss are part of the transition.

The general way to handle the emotions associated with a

move is this: once you are settled in to the new place, give your child space to be sad or angry and miss his old home (even if he loves his new one!). As the examples in this chapter show, letting go and missing the old is a necessary step toward coming together and embracing the new. Loss has to be recognized. For some children (and adults), the process takes time. Your child may focus on one seemingly small point to express their emotions about moving.

Four-year-old Laura cried each night when she went to sleep in her new house. "I miss the blue light outside my window. I can't sleep without it." Laura used to look at a blue light on the apartment building next door through her bedroom window. She thought of it as a night-light. Her parents talked to her about it, about how much she missed that light, and that sleeping in a new house felt funny. They gave her a narrative about their old house and bedroom and the new. They recognized her feelings of excitement but also sadness and worry. And then, one night, Laura unexpectedly announced, "I love my new bed. I like the purple sheets. And I don't like that blue light anyhow!" It takes time to adjust.

• New Baby •

The addition of a new sibling is big. It is exciting for the parents, but worrisome, too. It can also disrupt a child's sense of safety and security and the world as they know it. A new sibling is an upheaval for them.

One toddler, when told that his mother was going to have a baby soon, pondered this news. He then asked, "Who will be the baby's mommy?" When told that his mommy would be, but he would always be her first baby and her only

Liam, he stopped. He listened. Later, after his nap that day, he awoke with this pointed question: "Who decided you would be the baby's mommy?!"

Can you imagine sharing the one or two most important people in the world with someone else? Probably not. Becoming a big brother or sister brings up plenty of mixed feelings. Of course there is a lot of excitement. But children cannot be sure what it is all about. Will you still be my mommy? My daddy? Will you still love me? What is *really* inside mommy's belly? I think we, as parents, have a parallel set of mixed feelings, too. Letting go of the current family to welcome a new baby is also a change.

For your toddler, this trajectory of feelings is all extremely abstract. Your child goes from being your one and only (or if more than one child, maybe your toddler is the youngest, your baby right now) to being a big sibling, to sharing parents, to having a crying baby in the house. Imagine how confusing it is to your child. And the anticipation is usually the hardest part (for the parents, too!). That is why I stress that you wait and tell them as late in pregnancy as possible. Time is a concept they do not grasp. And the greater the lead time, the more anxiety that can set in.

Jade's parents could not wait to tell her about the new baby coming. As much as I encouraged them to wait until it was closer, they were sure she needed to know now. She was nearly four when her parents told her the news that in three months she would be a big sister. "I don't want to be a big sister," Jade responded. "I just want to be Jade." They reassured her that she would still be Jade, their biggest girl. But she would have none of it. "I am baby Jade now. We don't need more babies!" At other times, she announced what was hers and what she would not share. "Guess we will have to get another play room for that baby. This is *my* play room." She vacillated between being the big girl she liked to be and being a baby. She would lie on the floor, pretend to cry, and say, "I am the baby. Pick me up." One day she announced, "I am a very special baby. Very special. No new babies needed here."

Each morning when she awoke, she excitedly asked the same thing: "Is the new baby coming today?!" Of course, they had a long time to wait. For three months, the same question came nearly every day. And disappointment and anger followed when the answer was no. They came to see me because the day-to-day questioning of when the baby would come led to meltdowns, anger, and defiance. I suggested that they talk as little about the baby as possible, and tell Jade that the baby was not coming for a long, long time. Give her a focal point. When I was pregnant with my third baby, I told the older two that the baby would come after springtime started, when we had flowers and leaves on trees. Toddlers need a concrete frame—when winter starts and it is cold outside, after we have Christmas, after your school ends.

Often toddlers regress and show babyish behaviors as they anticipate the new baby coming (and after the arrival): whining, quick to cry, wanting to be held more, to play baby, and be rocked (even at four and five!). Indulge these needs for comfort and remind them, "You will always be my baby. Even when this tiny little new baby is here. You are always my baby, and we are always your mommy and daddy."

Once the baby is here, toddlers, even up to age five, will have lots of ambiguous feelings toward a new sibling—love/hate, aggression toward baby and mommy. I don't mean to say they won't love their sibling—it is truly a gift you are giving them. And when they show their love, it can be poignant and immense. But don't overlook that they also feel confused and misplaced. They are now sharing mommy and daddy, and jealousy is a natural feeling. Someone else is sharing in the attention they crave for themselves. Therefore they need continual reassurance that mommy and daddy still love them, will take care of them, and never lose sight of them in their hearts—no matter how many other siblings may join the family, and no matter what they are thinking or feeling about the new addition.

Preparing for the New Baby

A few weeks before the due date, but not too far ahead, explain to your child that soon the baby will be ready to come out. The key is to give them the basic plan so they have an idea of what will happen, but without too much detail. With all the excitement over a new baby, there is still one thing that matters most: their own well-being. So the main thing they want to know is that they will be cared for and okay and that you will still be their mommy and daddy. Too much information is overwhelming. Explain in clear and simple language that just like you did when he was born, mommy and daddy will go to the hospital and the doctor (or midwife) will help the baby come out. And then soon daddy and mommy will bring your new baby home. We will all be a family. Let him know who will stay when you go to the hospital, and assure your child that you will be back.

At our school we recommend that parents place a photo of the older child(ren) in the baby's bassinet. When your child visits at the hospital (and it is fine if you are not feeling up to it, they do not have to visit), their new brother or sister will be in the bassinet with the photo taped to the side. When my first child came to visit (he was twenty-three months), I showed him the photo in the bassinet and said, "Your new brother was looking at you. He wants to meet you." Make it all about your toddler, as if the baby were here only for them. For weeks at home, I'd say to my two-year-old, "Look! The baby is looking for you. He is smiling at you. He wants to know where his brother is," and so on. The baby was here in the service of his big brother and that made his brother feel part of it and important. Many parents have a gift from the new baby ready to give to the older sibling. My son had the stuffed monkey on his bed for years and called it his "Baby Monkey" because the baby gave it to him at the hospital.

What to Expect When the Baby Is Home

Yes, a new baby in the family is exciting. But from your child's point of view, it is not all it is cracked up to be. People may be saying, "Isn't it great that you are a big sister now? Your baby is so wonderful." And she may be thinking, *What's so great about it? Doesn't feel fun to me. Mommy is with baby. Baby cries a lot. Everyone is tired. Baby does not play. Not fun!* So, expect your child to behaviorally express how she likely feels inside. That can be acting out, tantrums, or most likely regression at some point. If she was toilet trained, she may be back to diapers or may have more accidents. Your child may wake up at night, even if she had not before. He may want to get in the baby's crib, play with the infant toys, or be rocked like a baby. He may become more possessive of his toys than he was in the past, grabbing and hoarding. "That's mine!" I often see children at the Toddler Center taking lots of crackers at snack time, as many as their hands can hold against their bodies, when there is an infant at home. Why? They feel intruded upon by the new family member and feel a strong desire to get everything they need. This passes in time.

What your child needs most is the comfort of knowing it is still okay to be a baby, your baby. By meeting these needs they will feel taken care of and better able to be the capable child they are. You can play baby games in a lighthearted and fun way with your child of any age. "Baby Fiona [who is four years old!] wants her bottle, here is a bottle for you tiny baby." Then in an equally fun way remind her, "Wait! Babies can't eat pizza or ice cream. You eat pizza and ice cream. You are my four-year-old Fiona! And my baby, too." She needs to feel baby and big without feeling ashamed at the mix of emotions inside of her.

The good news is that toddlers do like to help and be on the parental side. Even your two-year-old can be part of it. Ask them to grab a diaper or a burp cloth, and tell the baby that their sister or brother is helping take care of them. This empowers your child and provides them that sense of agency ("I have a role in this") that they thrive on.

And all those times you need to feed the baby, rock, pat, or put him to sleep? Remind your older one that as soon as you are done with the (feeding, diapering . . .), you will be able to play just with them. Find alone moments, even if it is just long enough to read a book together, or when you are putting your older one to sleep or driving to school. In these alone moments, highlight the exclusive time with your child. "It is only Mommy [or Daddy] and David right now. No baby here. She has to stay home. We'll see her later." Your child will relish these alone times. When toddlers come to our center, if there is a new baby or infant at home, we remind them, "There are no babies here. Your baby has to stay home; this school is only for you." The child usually lights up, often with a huge grin. He will then strut into school, feeling so big (and happy to be without that little baby for now). Later, when their baby arrives with Mommy or

Daddy at pickup, they often run and embrace their little sibling, happy to see them after a break.

When Will My Baby Play with Me?

Toddlers are all about "Me." I think the hardest part for toddlers is that from their point of view, newborns not only take attention away, they are simply dull and boring. There is lots of hype about a new baby coming, and then here is this baby who does very little as far your child is concerned. They cry, burp, poop, sleep, and steal attention, but they don't play! They are not fun! Connect to these feelings in your child. The more you can recognize the downside and negative feelings, the more freed they are to love their sibling—over time. Talk about a transition! Life was good before with just me and my parents. And now hours a day are spent waiting for Mommy, waiting for Daddy, deferring to the baby's needs, giving up what they had before. It is a loss. I spent much of my time saying to my older kids, "Oh, this baby is crying *again.* Can you believe it?" Or "He needs me to change him, *again.* Sure does need to be changed a lot." Your older one will likely give you a look of "Oh, she does get it. This *is* dull for me!" Let them know you understand what is on their mind and how they feel, that sometimes they like the baby and sometimes they don't. They will feel relieved, which frees them up to love their sibling, too, even if they can't always show it.

Aggression

It is understandable that children have some anger related to the new baby and the transition to being the "older" child. Remember, transitions stir a lot of emotions, and this is a particularly *big* transition. I find that if parents know that anger is possible (and likely!), they are less taken aback by it. Yes, the toddler loves the baby, their new sibling, and as they grow up together their relationship can blossom. No one shares a history like siblings do. And yes, they also are angry over the baby, their new sibling. Life was fine before and now there is an interloper. Some children get more upset than others. Some show it openly; some hold it in. There is often a honeymoon period before your child realizes that baby is here to stay for good. Many will do the hug-to-death-grip move where they hug the infant or newborn and the hug turns to an all-out squeeze. Keep your hands close to loosen the grip! But what this says is that your child has mixed feelings—it is love and it is anger, all tied together. Normal. As it should be.

It is not uncommon for children to show aggression—hitting, pushing, or biting—as an outlet for these mixed feelings after the birth of a new baby. It can happen soon after the baby is home or anytime in that first year. One mother called me and said, "He loves his newborn brother so much. He hugs him and says, 'Oh baby Will, I wuv you.' But then we go to the playground and he will randomly bite some child. He never showed aggression before, ever." But this is also a transition he has never weathered before. A father said to me, "Our toddler went from being a quiet and really good kid to one I am practically afraid to take anywhere. She is biting us or her baby sister, and if we are not vigilant, she can really hurt." And another parent said to me when her infant was six months old, "I thought we had sailed through the new-baby thing without any hitting or aggression. But now that the baby is sitting up, my older one is hitting me, so often. What is going on?!"

I don't mean to scare you. Aggression can worry or scare any parent. I understand why. But what is going on in these examples is normal at these ages. The three toddlers in the examples are all normal, healthy, and yes, sweet children. But adjusting to a new baby is fraught with ups and downs, and confusion. Underlying this are many mixed feelings they cannot understand. So be sure to recognize this and let them have outlets for it. "You can be angry at the baby. But I can't let you hurt her. Here is a doll [or pillow] that you can hit instead." If you can be accepting of the anger (which can be hard to do!), they will get more comfortable with it, too, and act out less. Sometimes parents worry that giving them a place to be angry—hitting a pillow or biting a doll or teddy bear—will increase their anger. I have never found that to be the case. In fact, just the opposite is true. When adults give them a contained place to be angry, it validates their anger and lets them know they are not alone. This brings their arousal and anger down, which actually helps them learn to manage the negative feelings and feel less upset.

• Starting School •

Going to school is another transition most young children face, whether it is their first school experience, returning after summer, or changing schools. They are used to the comforts of home, or the routines of the old school, or last year's classroom, and now they will start in a new place. Keep in mind that there is a lot to master in this transition. School presents all sorts of challenging newness: a new physical environment, new teachers and unknown classmates, new rules. A simple question such as "Where do I put my coat?" can be worrisome. *Who will comfort me if I miss mommy or daddy?* Think about your own experiences. Do you recall starting a new job and having the anxiety over where you would go for lunch, or where the bathroom was? Toddlers feel this way. There are new adults to build relationships with, new children to get to know, and a room with routines they have to learn. It leaves them feeling unsteady until they can settle in. It can be scary, even if it is fun. The phase-in period that most preschools offer does give your child time to get acclimated with the room, materials, routines, people, and most important, to build trust with the adult caregivers so they feel safe in your absence. All children differ in their reactions to starting school: Some enter new schools like they've been there before, eager to engage and try it all out. Others hold back, observe, and take their time. They may feel most comfortable watching and standing close to you. All manners of starting school are fine; children's approaches and paces vary. Even the toddler who bounds into school with excitement, eager to try out new activities on day one, may react many weeks later to his parent leaving. So regardless of their style, transitions take time.

Preparing Your Child

Prepare your child for the new school experience, but don't overdo it. Sometimes parents get so excited about a new school that they want to tell their child right away. It could be April and they say to a two- or three-year-old, "In September you will be going to a new school!" September? That is a lifetime away. Instead, a week or two before school begins, tell your child that they will be starting a new school soon. You could drive by or play on the playground so they can see where it is. If they visited in the spring, remind them of that. If you know the teachers' names, tell them. Maybe the teacher will even come to visit. And name a few activities they might do at school (play with blocks, sing songs, climb at the playground). Assure them that you will take them and stay for the first few days. As I've said earlier, the main point is that your children will want to know that you are coming back. So when you do leave them at school for the first time (and the days after), let them know when they will see you again, marked by a concrete event (time is meaningless at these ages): "I will be back to pick you up after music time," or "Daddy will pick you up and I will see you at dinner." Separation at school is a big deal—they are in a new place without you. When they master that, they feel great. It is a big step toward independence. You've helped them over an important hurdle. What allows them to succeed in your absence is knowing that you will be back!

But in the meantime, much of their emotional energy goes into handling the separation, whether they show that outwardly or not, so expect regression at home. Regression can include more whining or demanding behaviors, increased clinginess, crying more readily, or disruption in sleep. All of this tells you that they are working hard to master separation, even several months into the school year.

• • •

Whether large transitions or everyday ones, we parents need to keep in mind that from a toddler's perspective, transitions are tough. They don't just happen; they present challenges to master. Toddlers are not yet ready to take them in stride and "roll with the punches." Some are more able than others, but they all need our help. We need to be there for them as they go from the ending of one moment (playing, bath, leaving home), through the transition, to the beginning of the next. We need to be patient as we watch them wrestle with their discomfort and wrap their growing brains around the task of getting used to change. As they grow, have more experiences, and their brains mature, they will gain better skills for anticipating what comes next, planning and organizing, and understanding and handling their emotional responses to change. These are essential pieces for managing transitions. As these structures are put in place, your child will gradually get better at managing transitions on their own. Out of this comes good feelings about what they can do and how they can handle life. Remember that in the beginning, at two or three years old, or even at four and five, the way toddlers manage transitions won't be perfect, and they'll rely heavily on us as parents to guide them. Just when you think they have mastered transitions, the next day they can backslide, reminding us of how much we are needed.

Helping toddlers with these transitions requires us to provide structure, empathy, and a flexible reliance on routine. In the midst of this intense emotional reality, toddlers need to know they are okay, even if they feel unsteady as change hap-

---

Parenting POV
Understanding Transitions

Think of your own transitions. An adult parallel to the toddler transition can feel like this: It's Friday afternoon and you and your partner have plans to go to an evening party. You've been looking forward to it as a nice way to end a hectic week. Even if you *want* to go to a party and see your friends, you may have some anxiety about getting there, starting the conversation—getting to what is new. "Who will be there?" you may ask yourself. You may feel tired and wonder if you have energy to revive yourself and be social. But once there, you know you will enjoy it. Yet, the hurdle is in dragging yourself there. What does the anticipation of the party or event feel like to you? Excitement? Pleasure? Anxiety? Dread? A mix of all four? These feelings are similar to what your toddler feels, even at transitions to something they want to do!

---

pens. Just as we need to help calm them when they are upset in more extreme circumstances, it is also our role to be there reminding them that they are not alone and that it is okay to be having trouble leaving home, saying good-bye to grandma, getting into pajamas, or losing a tooth.

Like most challenges of the toddler years, helping your child learn to manage transitions with more ease plays an important role in how your child navigates changes—big and small—in the future. It also lays down the tracks for being more flexible. In this way, when you help your child become confident about his or her own ability to manage transitions, despite their difficulty, they internalize confidence: *This is tough but I can do it.* And that's resilience!

Cue In to Toddler POV

Remember, helping your children to learn to manage transitions on their own means first understanding the world from their vantage point. This lens provides the context for understanding the seemingly wacky and zany world they live in (it is truly not the same colored glasses that the adults are wearing). Their world is colored by and bathed in innocence and wonder, a need for immediate gratification, no sense of time or what comes next, and lots of change within themselves. So the first step is to understand this. Yet that does not mean giving in to their every desire. In fact, the opposite is true: helping a child function in *spite* of their constant and changing desires. But understanding the context of their world helps frame their behavior and needs in ways more understandable to the adult. Once you get this, then you can figure out what to do. To guide the child into our world, meaning socialization of the child, we have to move into theirs first, see it from their point of view.

chapter eight

Cracking the Code on Toddler Learning

Play, Sharing, and Leaving Children Alone

"Jump in the boat," calls Jordana. "There is an emergency and we have to hurry!"

Michael and Reyna jump in the wooden rocking boat.

"I am the doctor with the shots," calls Reyna.

"I have the medicine," Michael responds.

"I don't like yukky medicine," adds Jordana.

"It will make you feel better," Dr. Reyna tells her.

The children rock back and forth until one of the four-year-olds insists they have arrived.

"Not yet," calls out Michael, and they all agree to rock more. Soon they are there.

"The sick dog is over here," Jordana says, pointing to a stuffed animal on the floor.

The three tumble out of the boat and scurry over to the stuffed animal in need of their care. "Let's build a bed for the dog," Jordana suggests as she takes out rectangular and square blocks and hands them to her two friends nearby.

"Can I help?" asks Niya, entering into the play scenario.

"Yeah, we need help," the friends respond. Blocks fall over until they figure out how to build the bed steadily. The stuffed animal is delicately placed inside to rest.

Their busy play enacts pieces of the adult world as well as their life experiences, while empowering them to be in charge.

These are children engaged in their surroundings, using all of its contents to their delight, mimicking the language and phrases of the adults with whom they interact on a daily basis, and acting out situations and learning how to do things "all by myself!" In the example above, these children are four years old. They have learned how to play with one another, negotiate roles, and cooperate. If they were younger, two or three years old, they might not be able to manage such a sophisticated imaginary game yet. Still, they'd be at the beginning of pretend play. But by four, they are off to the races.

Understanding why play is so important to toddlers not only helps us see inside the child's world and understand their point of view but also offers a valuable lens on how children actually learn. Indeed, current research in the brain and cognitive sciences agrees that it is learning that truly spurs development. And young children learn most when they are at play.

Why does this matter? Because all too often, parents are

hearing more and more about how to speed up their child's learning, as if you can fast-track them to Harvard by offering young children foreign language lessons, piano or violin, advanced ballet or gymnastics, and teaching them how to read at two! All before they are even old enough to enter elementary school! In many places today, the messages about what is good for children put pressure on parents that work against children's best interests and future success. Parents are told young children need direct teaching and lessons up front. In fact, children's natural inclination is to learn. They are born with curiosity, wonder, and excitement about people and the world around them. They are born with a drive to learn through their own discoveries and exploration. Directive and rule-bound lessons work against this natural inclination. Instead, the adults' task in toddler learning is supporting their inherent drive and curiosity, the basis for developing motivation and interest in learning. Developmental and educational research studies support this idea, that nurturing children's inherent drive, curiosity, and desire to explore creates problem solvers and thinkers.

When children play, they are learning how the world works—figuring it out by taking initiative. They learn how to carry out transactions. How to communicate. How to navigate their way through situations and problem-solve. Play teaches children about themselves, others, rules, consequences, and how things go together or come apart. Play builds their sense of agency—that they have an impact on their environment, they can make things happen. Agency is connected to self-confidence, and both are related to self-regulation. I commonly watch toddlers gather and collect toys. What looks like hoarding from an adult view is collecting to the toddler: it's as if they are thinking, *I need to get everything I need. This is mine.* Collecting allows the toddler to feel secure, that she has what she needs. This builds confidence as they figure out what they need and how to obtain it. After this fulfillment is reached a child can begin to see what others need. She can also identify what she likes or dislikes. One child collects cars; another picks up Lego blocks or even pipe cleaners. Each collection defines the child. My own toddler took a different toy animal with him to school most days and by age four had developed an interest in whales. At ten he continues to be a passionate lover of whales, one who now reads about and studies them and has dreams of becoming a marine biologist. The interest and passion first emerged as a toddler.

Two-and-a-half-year-old Olivia is riding on a toy truck. "I working," she firmly states.

She carefully places blocks onto the truck in a stack, focused with deep concentration. They fall and she begins anew. "This one fits, but this one doesn't fit."

She picks up more small blocks. "I don't like the blue ones. Only red ones."

As she carefully works to make these blocks fit together, she mutters, "I very busy now. Very busy."

"Just playing" provides her the opportunity to figure it out—how to make the blocks fit. Fitting the blocks uses spatial and mathematical concepts; it builds problem-solving skills and the ability to handle frustration. She is figuring out her likes and dislikes and feeling empowered by being involved in "work" just like the adults around her do. How good that feels to a toddler! At the same time, she is practicing vocabulary, stating colors and imitating what she observes in the adult world. So much learning happens in this one play episode.

So if play is so important, why do many people still tend to think of it as the opposite of work, and therefore frivolous? Play is often trivialized, in sayings like "That is mere child's play" or "He is only playing," as if to say play is unimportant and not a serious endeavor. Many would prefer that young children spend their time tracing letters, obediently following adult directions, or matching figures on a worksheet. But this view of play is an adult view. It reflects an adult misunderstanding of what learning is—not looking at the world through the eyes (or brain) of a toddler and for that reason only offers a judgmental, inaccurate, and unrealistic way of thinking about toddler learning.

Of course, it should come as no surprise that the Toddler Center is based upon the notion that if you place young children in a stimulating, safe environment that is set up for their exploration, supporting them as necessary, then they will naturally engage with their world, explore, discover, and, yes, learn. And that is the essence of play.

For toddlers, there is no line between learning and playing. Learning is all about play. From morning to night, upon waking until laying their sleepy heads down (finally) at day's end, a toddler has a one-track mind: What can I do? What can I discover? What can I explore? I like to think of toddlers as scientists: in their exploratory stage of life, they are trying out and discovering what is around them, delighting in all that they can touch, see, smell, hear, and even taste. They have their hands and fingers, toes and tongues into everything that triggers their curiosity. They don't have to be taught how to play—it's as natural as breathing the air. Their curiosity is insatiable. As a parent, you likely know that, since it is hard to keep them from touching, discovering, and exploring, even when you try! Playing is what they are meant to do, all the while growing and developing in mind, brain, body, and spirit. Recent neuroscience findings validate this view. Pretend play and self-exploration are essential to developing those important executive function skills I wrote about in earlier chapters. Executive function skills include problem solving, planning, flexibility in setting up a new plan, creativity, persistence, and managing emotions. These are skills built directly out of the kinds of open-ended play toddlers engage in and are also bedrocks of lifelong success.

And yet, in this addled age of making sure our kids turn out to be perfect (ahem), parents and schools can get carried away with pushing young children beyond what is developmentally appropriate—all in the name of enrichment and accelerated learning. In this chapter, I want to share with you not only my philosophy about how kids learn best but why this is so. I also want to shed some light on the nature of learning and what really matters for your current child and *future* student—and it doesn't involve learning Mandarin as a second language (unless that is your home language) at age three, four, or five!

• What Does Play Look Like? •

Although there is no one, universal definition of play, there are certain agreed-upon aspects that characterize the way all children play. First, when children are playing, they are enjoying themselves. They look happy, at ease, at peace, or sometimes very exhilarated. Psychologists call this positive state of mind *positive affect,* which points to a kind of emotional temperature. Second, when kids play they are *engaged.* They are attentive, involved, and not easily distracted from what they are doing. They are naturally involved in whatever the activity is—without the need for reward, directive, or pressure. They want to play for the sheer pleasure of playing. You may wonder how something so pleasure-driven can be called learning. Active engagement, fueled by the pleasure the child feels, becomes the basis for focus and persistence in your future student. Third, and closely related to engagement and enjoyment, is perhaps the most widely agreed-upon aspect of play—a child's intrinsic, or internal, motivation to play. Different factors can motivate a child: novelty, gaining a new angle on a familiar experience, achieving mastery with known objects (think of all those times your child has repeated the same activity or action over and over again), needing to work through feelings. Although the motivation comes from the child, adults establish a safe environment and support or assist in the play, if needed by the child.

Fourth, they are *unencumbered by the rules* of others. In many ways, the child's play world lives outside the adult world. Almost anything is possible as imaginations soar, and their logic is different from ours. What does this aspect of play mean for your child's learning and future development? Creativity, vision, and innovation, qualities that employers now complain are highly lacking in recent college graduates. Children may make up their own logic or rules of a game, but they are not at all concerned with how to follow the rules of adults. The rules today may be different from yesterday. Watch young children play. The rules are set, negotiated, changed, and renegotiated, even if the rules seem odd to the adult.

Millie is holding a ball and refuses to throw it. Larson calls, "But you have to throw it. That's the rule. Throw it!" Millie responds, "First, you stand and hold it. I am holding it. I have it so I get to decide when to throw." "Okay," concedes Larson. "I get to hold it long when I have it, too."

In free play, rules shift, too. Rhea, who is the mommy in the game, states, "You can't take all the blocks. Only the mommy gets all the blocks." Aishah counters, "I'm the baby. The baby can have all of them, too."

But freedom from external rules does not mean the total absence of rules. Children set their own rules, governing roles, relationships, entry into play, plot development, and acceptable behaviors. The players develop and agree upon the rules, which are implicitly understood.

It's cleanup time, and the pizza delivery girl makes an entry. "Who ordered a pepperoni pizza?" Texeira hollers as she carries a block toward the block shelf.

"I did," answers Ashook as he takes the block from Texeira and places it on the shelf. He is the block organizer, neatly stacking the wooden "pizzas" according to size.

Soon other children begin delivering pizza. As they pass the blocks to Ashook, the chants echo through the classroom: "Who ordered a cheese pizza?" "Here's another pizza!"

The children have distributed roles and created a structure for their pretend play to succeed. While the activity leads to a successful cleanup, the pretend aspects are what engage the children and sustain the play. And in addition to learning new vocabulary and completing a task, they are learning to work together as a team—another highly regarded twenty-first-century skill.

Finally, when young children play, they focus on the process or performance of the activity, not on a goal or the results. This is why play is play and work is work. When we work, even when we enjoy work, we are not only aware of our process, we are also motivated by its outcome—getting paid, earning an award, reaching a set goal. It is this aspect in part that separates play from work. When young children play, the activity is all about the process—there is no separation between the two. And it is through this process that learning and development take place. As children work together or figure things out through play, they build confidence in their abilities. Confidence allows children to take chances, learn, and grow. It is this confidence, derived through play, that they take into academic learning as they get older—a feeling of excitement about figuring it out, whether it is learning to add or read new words.

Although adults establish and guide the play environment, whether at home or in a school environment such as the Toddler Center, children are meant to feel free and autonomous so they can initiate play in whatever form. In this way, the environment where children play is very important; it gives safe guidelines for where they can play. A room that feels cheerful, offers options with developmentally appropriate toys, and a choice of materials (for example, sand, water, paint, pretend props) significantly facilitates the process of play. Children do not need many toys or materials in order to play. In fact, fewer materials tend to facilitate more play because children can create meaning from the materials at hand without being overwhelmed or distracted by excessive options. In your own home, look around. Do you have too many toys? I frequently suggest that parents put away half the toys in their house. They are amazed at how much more engaged their child becomes.

What to Do

Toddlers are explorers. They want to touch, taste, smell, listen to, throw, and sometimes eat objects in order to gain information about an object. This "operation curiosity" becomes the foundation that often leads to play. This same curiosity, if nurtured, is what excites them about learning throughout their educational experience. In exploration children ask, "What is this? What can it do? What can *I* do with it?" As parents, we can help this inquiry process by following up on our child's lead in a nonintrusive but supportive way that can guide her play. As your child pushes his train on the wooden track and says, "It's going to grandma's," you can comment, "I wonder what the train will do when it gets there." As your child picks up mounds of wet mud and mushes it between her hands, a comment like "I wonder what that feels like" cues her in to the sensation and extends her experience. When we interact with our children in this supportive way, following their lead, adults invite children into a space in which they will feel comfortable exploring, discovering things that are familiar, and developing feelings of competence and security.

• How Does Play Support Learning and Development? •

Enrichment and growth naturally evolve from playing as children learn about themselves and their surroundings. A child's active participation in his or her world facilitates mastery and control, leading to feelings of competence and self-efficacy, and these characteristics are the foundation of the successful future student. Without a belief in their own competence as they are learning new things, no student will persist or keep trying in spite of mistakes. As children "figure it out" through their play—as Olivia did when the blocks did not fit on her truck in the earlier example—they begin to feel they can solve problems. They can work it out. And by doing so, children become even more curious, more excited about trying things out (a skill needed later when they approach new learning, such as learning multiplication for the first time or trying to decode the sounds of letters), and more sure that they will succeed if they keep trying possible ways of doing it. This is persistence, a key factor in academic success. The child who feels good about her ability to figure things out, to solve the problem—whether that is fitting the piece into a five-piece puzzle, balancing the final block on top of an unsteady tower, or negotiating a way for three people to fit into the rocking boat that only holds two—develops the base for becoming a motivated and self-assured learner, one who feels confident in her ability to succeed.

This sense of competence and belief in oneself becomes the passion that drives the older learner. Play lets children make important discoveries about the self—including their own likes and dislikes and what they can and cannot do. They continually shift activities to maximize pleasure, while discovering what is easy and hard to do and what makes them happy or frustrated. They learn to understand the feelings of others and develop empathy. These skills are also crucial for healthy peer relationships and showing compassion. Children who are tuned in to others' feelings and emotions are more successful in friendships and social interactions. Positive social interactions are tied to later success in school, more positive attitudes in life, and success in careers as adults.

And for the toddler, this sense of competence and control over her world is deeply related to her sense of safety. So while children are playing from morning to night, they are also constantly working out, often through play, the struggle between independence and the need for security.

Julia, nearly three, cries at her mother's departure. "It's okay to cry when you're sad," the teacher quietly reassures the child slumped in her lap. "Mommies and daddies always come back."

Two-year-old Harry, perched on a chair nearby, closely watches the scene. He wiggles off the chair, slowly approaches Julia, and hands her a teddy bear. Harry repeats the teacher's mantra: "Mama come back soon." He hands her the toy that brings him comfort—a step toward true empathy.

Play also fosters language skills. Pretend play encourages language development as children negotiate roles, set up a structure, and interact in their respective roles. Adults support language by commenting on or labeling children's play ("I see you are washing that baby," "That's a big blue painting you're making!"). Such comments provide a language-rich environment and naturally reinforce concepts (big-little; more-less; over-under; colors or shapes) and build on the play. Language is also tied to emotions, which are expressed and explored through pretend play. Pretending gives children the freedom to address feelings, anxieties, and fears, and as we know, children need our help not squashing these negative emotions but managing them. That is why fantasy and imaginary games are so important. They let children re-create and modify experiences to their liking, helping them gain a sense of control over a situation; this leads again to a sense of comprehension and mastery. This can enhance feelings of security, which are so important to toddlers as they separate and look to discover their true selves. Think back to the children who were playing doctor to the hurt puppy. Rather than going to the doctor themselves, which can be frightening, they became the doctor, the one who gives shots and forces medicine, allowing them to handle hard feelings. Next time they are sick, the doctor visit may be less scary.

Pretend also gives children a way to push through emotionally challenging situations.

"Hop-hop!" announces Jamal as he hops into the room, hiding his head in his arm. "Today froggy is here."

Last week when he entered he crawled in. "Raaaahhhhh!" he fiercely announced. "A tiger is at school today."

Another time, he wore a cape. "Super boy is at school!"

Each of these characters gives Jamal the ability to become a more powerful or brave being, allowing him to put aside the timid child who fears leaving his mother. Instead, being a jumpy frog, a fierce animal, or a super boy lets him test the waters and helps him cross into the classroom with confidence. If he is supported in these emotional needs, then in time the frog or tiger or super boy will disappear and Jamal will enter the classroom as himself. When he is ready. Play gives him the capacity to handle these hard emotions at his own pace.

Parents or caregivers have an important role in reinforcing and supporting the play. Labeling feelings and reflecting on emotional content is an effective way to extend fantasy play: "That tiger sounds so angry." It can help children understand feelings and develop empathy by saying, "Why do you think that monster is so sad?" Play is a vehicle for expressing feelings, with minimal language needed as the child acts out the pretend character. Moving feelings from the child to the pretend character reduces anxiety and frees the child to explore emotions. Children will "try on" emotions through the roles they play (as baby, mommy, or daddy, as firefighter, monster, tiger, or doctor) and through puppets or other toy animals.

One day, a three-year-old at our center who was having a hard time saying good-bye to her mother at dropoff picked up a puppet. She put it on her hand and stated, "He's happy. So happy," and then immediately after, "He's sad now. Very sad." She repeated this sequence over and over as a way to express her desire to separate (happy) and the sadness in leaving mommy. "Maybe he is sad because he misses his mommy. She will still come back," the teacher responded. The adult's message is "It is safe to have and express these feelings."

So, what do emotions have to do with learning? Everything. Persistence, taking on new challenges and risks, handling frustration, the ability to focus for long periods of time, are all tied to being able to manage emotions. Not giving up on something, on solving a problem or figuring out a solution (puzzle, building a tower, or a complicated math problem), means pushing through even when it is hard and frustration seeps in. It is the ability to handle the emotions that arise during challenges. These are the skills that researchers and educators alike have identified as essential to learning (and as too often lacking in our students), above and beyond one's intellectual capacity. You can be smart, but if you can't manage emotions enough to persevere, or you are preoccupied with negative feelings, then success is hard to obtain.

Now, I don't mean to misguide you. For toddlers, persistence is in the making. They will persist at desires of their own (as when they want candy or a coveted toy) but not necessarily at tasks you view as important. Fear not! I see it often at our center. Toddlers start a puzzle or other problem-oriented toy and when they can't figure it out they walk away. I don't view this as giving up, because I know they will come back to it, whether the same day or maybe a week or two later. And when they eventually figure it out, they will be excited. That is what fuels persistence.

• Owning and Sharing •

Two-year-olds cannot be expected to share, because they do not yet fully understand that others have wishes that could conflict with their own. They only know what they want, at this moment, and what they want is "mine." Their job is to first figure out what ownership means. This will soon start to change as they begin to play with peers. Three- and four-year-olds are getting better at sharing because they have a more developed sense of what is "mine," but they, too, can get confused and act in ways that appear selfish to us. At these ages, children don't have a sense of time, which also makes sharing a nearly impossible task. Before they can share, they have to understand "You have it now, I have it at a later time." What they desire, they desire now. What does all this mean? Don't expect kids this age to share willingly, genuinely, or generously . . . they just don't get it yet. They are not being rude or mean. They simply can't understand. Children who are pushed to share too soon remain selfish until much older ages. A shift begins starting around age three or three and a half when children become more interested in peers and want to make friends. Sharing starts to come naturally then, but still won't happen all the time!

What to Do

These days sharing is a loaded topic. Adults insist on it even when children are not ready for it. Sharing is hardest at home, since these are possessions that belong to your child and on his home turf. If you are having another child over, let your child put away one or two (or three!) favorite toys so there are no battles. Set up activities that the children can do together—

Loving a Lovey

Some kids become especially attached to an object—a blanket, a stuffed animal, sometimes a book or a favorite baseball mitt—that they take with them wherever they go. Even items such as a key chain or toothbrush can be the lovey. Such loveys or transitional objects help kids as they learn to self-soothe, regulate their feelings, and work out their fears during times of transition. It is a familiar piece of home that provides security in a big world. It is the toddler equivalent of the adult good luck charm. A little piece that reminds them of home and brings comfort.

stacking blocks, puzzles, art activity. If conflicts happen over a much-desired toy, see if the children can work it on their own (they often do when adults don't interfere). Conflict is a natural part of playing together. It is part of learning to work it out. If not, you may have to distract and change activities, go outside, or take a snack break. Playdates for two-year-olds are better outside or on other neutral territories. They get better at it over time! Three- to five-year-olds are better able to play together and work out conflicts, but not all the time. Keep playdates short, no more than two hours. And only one playmate at a time. Three, I assure you, is a crowd. And what if your child is possessive, crying and whining, and unhappy throughout the playdate? It has happened to all of us, myself included. Cut it short. There is always a next time.

• Learning to Share •

Just like any aspect of development, learning does not happen in a vacuum. It is the result (or outcome) of social interaction—between children, between parent and child, between child and teacher. This is how children eventually learn that "even though I like peanut butter and jelly sandwiches, Sue Ellen doesn't," that "I hate to go down the slide really fast, but Mark loves it!" Throughout the toddler years, young children are beginning to hone an important cognitive skill called theory of mind. Though there is some discussion about when children actually develop theory of mind, most psychologists and educators agree that it's during the toddler years when theory of mind becomes important to learning, especially in terms of how children begin to understand who they are, how they are different from other children, and how they are able to manage and direct themselves. In other words, once children understand that other people have different thoughts and feelings, they are able to differentiate themselves and develop a sense of unique identity—related to the sense of agency we talked about in the last chapter.

So what does this have to do with sharing? Everything. Sharing seems to be an important goal nearly all parents have for their children. You likely want that for your child. I certainly do. But not at these ages, and not consistently, even at age five (when they are getting better at it). We may all wish for our children to be kind and compassionate people who want to share. But sharing is more than simply handing over an object. It is an ability that evolves over time and has social and emotional underpinnings. So here's the catch: Wishing for it, and forcing it upon your child by saying, "Share, share" doesn't make it so. Just the opposite; it backfires. Forcing a child to share asks them to *give up something* that is theirs at this moment. *Deprive me of what I need?* Most of us wouldn't choose to be deprived, which is what forced sharing feels like to a toddler. Insistence on sharing comes at a time when their whole being is figuring out who they are and what they need, when their main focus is *Me* and *Mine*. Forcing a child at this age to share makes them incapable of sharing for much longer. Really.

Why? Because true sharing is an act of altruism—it comes from an emotional base, from the heart. It is a desire to give to others, to be generous. Before a child can be genuinely altruistic and able to include others in what they have, she must first feel deep inside herself that her own needs are met. The toddler also needs to know that giving to another does not mean forfeiting her own needs in the future. Remember how toddlers live in the present? The two- or three-year-old sense of time is a continuous now; they have little sense of yesterday or tomorrow—the future is an abstraction that they literally don't understand. Because of this warped sense of time, they also are just beginning to hold on to the belief and the feeling that when mommy goes away she's really coming back. In the moment, no matter how many times they are told, two- and three-year-olds don't quite trust the coming-back part. They can be distracted, or quieted down by a teacher or caregiver. But that is not the same as understanding and holding in their minds the idea that mommy leaves and returns. Four- and five-year-olds are bridging this conceptual-emotional gap.

So when it comes to sharing, the toddler does not have the confidence or trust that it's okay to give something away. They have no understanding that they can ever get it back. Throughout these years, just as they are learning that their friends are different from themselves, they are also gradually learning how to trust that their own internal needs are manageable. Only then are they able to see what other people want and need. In today's overzealous child-rearing culture, the word *share* has taken on a life of its own. Sharing is equated with being a decent person. That may fit for adults but it is far from fitting for young children. Misunderstanding what sharing is and how your child learns about it over time gets in the way of healthy social development. This is especially true if *share* means giving up what they have and need. People who feel deprived or in need of something do not feel generous, especially when they are two, three, four, or five.

It may surprise you just how complicated the act of sharing actually is. Adults insist to children, "Just share." For the toddler, there is nothing *just* in sharing. What is just to them is when they have, hold, touch, or hoard everything they want. It won't always be this way, and it gets better as they move past three and closer to five. But for now that is who they are and how it must be. It can be embarrassing for you (a civilized adult) when your child does not readily give up what they have to others, when your child holds on with all his might. Before you know it, they will genuinely partake in this altruistic exchange, but only *if* you let them act like toddlers now—in all its selfish-seeming ways.

If we unravel the pieces needed before one can genuinely share, then it becomes clear why toddlers can't. What is needed to share? A sense of: self and mine; ownership; their needs getting met ("I have all I need, now I can look around and see what others need"); other people and their feelings (which can be different from their own); time (for turn-taking); patience, control of actions, and ability to override impulses (waiting; not grabbing what they want).

So why do toddlers stubbornly refuse to share? The simple answer is, *they can't.*

Two-year-olds cannot be expected to share, because they

do not yet fully understand that others have wishes that could conflict with their own. They only know what they want, at this moment, and what they want is "mine." Toddlers are in the throes of understanding ownership for the first time: "This is *mine*!" They view objects as part of who they are, which you know because they hold on for dear life to anything they label "mine." This part can worry parents, as it looks so selfish from the adult view. So I will remind you that they don't stay at this stage forever; still, it is one they must pass through. As their brains develop and they begin to get a sense of others as people, too, they enter the realm of peers. And that is when they start to get better at cooperation and sharing. But first the toddler's job is to figure out what ownership means. This will gradually change as they begin to play with peers. When they want to make friends, they have more motivation to share. Three- and four-year-olds are getting better at sharing because they have a more developed sense of what is "mine" and a more developed sense of "others" but they often get confused and act in ways that appear selfish to us. When adults give them the support and distance to work it out, more often than not, they do.

At these ages, children have no or little sense of time, which also makes sharing nearly impossible. Even when they say "in five minutes!" what they mean is "not now." Giving up what they have in the framework of "it is his turn" or "your turn will be next" requires a sense of time. To the toddler, these are arbitrary rules made up by the powerful adults. In truth, what toddlers desire, they desire now.

Then there is the desire to help others. Toddlers, especially at two, have little understanding of what others think and feel. That comes later. What they know is Me. The idea that someone else desires what *I* have is incomprehensible. *I have it, I want it. End of story.*

What does all this mean? Again, don't expect kids this age to share willingly, genuinely, or generously . . . they just don't get it yet. They are not being rude or selfish. They simply cannot understand in any real or sincere way. Their brains do not yet have that capacity.

The parent says, "Share with your friend. He just wants a turn." The young child hears "You can no longer have what you need and desire. I am forcing you to give it away. And I expect you to do so nicely." How does the toddler feel? Terrible. Ashamed. For having a desire he is being told to let go of. Instead, try this. You can cue your three- or four-year-old into the other child and their desire, without shaming your own child for what he needs: "Jose also wants to play. So when you are done, let us know. Jose is waiting." We do this at our center, and what it does, even at age two, is tell the child they can have their desire to keep playing met, but it introduces the idea of other children and other children's desires. But it makes no demands on the child to give up what they have.

One day at the Toddler Center, three-year-old Luis was playing with a truck. Although there was another one just like it, his friend Marielle, two and a half, wanted what he had. She tried several times to take it, but he held on to it, screaming, "I'm playing! I have it!" A teacher nearby came over and said, "I see you are playing. It looks like Marielle wants to play, too. When you are finished, she can play." He settled down, held it close to his chest, and quietly said, "I'm just busy now. I am not finished yet." The teacher responded and validated his need: "That's fine. Play as long as you need. And when you are done, Marielle will be waiting." He played, but within minutes, on his own, he graciously handed it over to his friend. Why? Because once his need was validated, and there was no pressure put on him, he was willing to share with a friend.

Added to this is a lack of control over impulses. If they want something, especially at ages two and three, they are likely to grab. Having the patience to wait for what they want is a milestone during these years. Helping them wait, to delay gratification ("I know you want that ball and it is hard to wait. But when he is done, you can have it.") is an important role of adults. Their brains and bodies get better at waiting (part of the executive function skills) but they need our help in learning it. When the children arrive at our center, they wait in a hall outside the classroom. It is hard for them to wait—they bang on the door or pull on the knob. My mantra to them is "Your teachers are getting all the toys ready. But they are *so slow.* It is so hard to wait. Hurry up, teachers! Let's hold on tight, they'll be here soon." The children will stop banging, look at me, laugh, or feel calmer. As soon as the door opens, they dash inside—the triumph of having waited! I have helped them manage the frustration of waiting. A step toward better self-control. Only to be repeated the next time they come. Learning to wait takes practice.

It all sounds fairly selfish, I know—just as it needs to be for a first step. They want what they want; they want it now and on their own terms. The hardest piece to imagine is this: If we help our children feel like they have what they need at two and three and four, and that includes holding on to toys and objects they are playing with, then they become generous and giving. Later. Sharing and generosity emerge out of his loving relationship with you, when you respond to his needs. It comes from your helping her handle limits and frustration and gradually learn to delay gratification. She begins to know that she cannot always get what she wants right away. Being able to wait, to not have their desire met right away, makes them better able to share and do the give-and-take of socializing ("You play with this now, and I play with it when you're done").

As they move from ages two to five they are also becoming more aware of social rules and expectations. Based in a loving relationship with you, they actually *do* want to please you (I know it doesn't always seem this way). And they do so partly by meeting these adult-set social expectations (such as sharing), at least some of the time.

I often encounter the following "sharing" scenario. A three-year-old turns to a friend who has a doll or something he wants and says, "Share. Share with me." What he means is "Give that to me. I want it." They have learned that share means give-it-away. And his self-focused nature to meet his own need of the moment moves him to demand the toy be given over; it's his interpretation of sharing.

One day I went to a playground with my youngest child, accompanied by a friend and his daughter. My little one, at three, and with two older siblings, had learned to hold on tightly for what he needed. His friend was an only child. They walked to the park and he carried two buckets with two shovels, as I wanted to be sure there was enough for the other child. But he was not letting go. She quietly asked, "Can I have one?"

"No," my toddler responded (thrilled to have them both and not have any brothers around to take one). He trotted onward.

Soon she tried again. "Can I have a bucket?" He sweetly responded, "No."

Now I felt the eyes of the father on me, wanting me to do something so his child could have a toy. Pressure! I commented that maybe soon he would let her have one (I did not say "share," as I knew that for my son, it would be giving something up).

Next, she turned to him and with a little more vigor said, "Share with me. It's time to *share* with me!"

Sharing meant "give me." An altruistic act? Likely not. And he still did not.

Then, as soon as we arrived at the park, he turned and gave her a bucket and shovel. On his own terms, at his own pace. The two played together in the sandbox, no adults needed.

By the next year in pre-K, the reports we had from teachers were of how kind and thoughtful he was with other children, and this is the feedback we continue to get many years later.

My point is that he learned to hold on to what he needed first, and that allowed him to be generous to others. Give them the chance and they get there. Is it embarrassing, in the meantime, to watch your child holding on to what they have and not generously sharing it with others? It can be, especially with other parents staring at you. Yet one of the most common issues parents raise with me (especially with firstborns!) is their concern that their child cannot hold on to what they want. As soon as another child approaches them, they will give up what they have. That is the flip side, a child who does not yet have the strength to stand up for their needs. A child who repeatedly has things taken from them.

As for your seemingly selfish child who is rarely capable of sharing? I promise that this can change. Two-year-olds play in tandem with peers, imitating their actions. Starting around age three, they get more interested in peers; soon after they want to make friends, get along with peers, and be liked. The motivation to share begins, first on their own terms and then more altruistically over time. Sharing starts to come naturally in this context as they negotiate with other children and work out conflicts, but it still won't happen all the time!

Even as children become more generous and learn to share, there will be lots of bumps in the road and exceptions. Sharing tends to be hardest in their own home. Home has possessions that belong to your child. Home belongs to them. And if another child comes over, their territory is being entered. It may feel intrusive to your child, which makes them more possessive and less likely to share. This is especially true if there are other events going on in their life—an infant sibling, out-of-town visitors, mommy or daddy away, getting over a recent cold.

Conflicts will happen—it is a natural part of children's interactions. Step back and give children the opportunity to work it out on their own. Working it out is part of peer play, and a good skill to learn. Conflict requires problem solving, and problem solving is necessary for learning. Handling conflicts also boosts your child's confidence that they can work out problems.

But what about when the playdate just falls apart? Your child can't share anything. Conflicts abound. That will happen, too.

Layla, almost three, was excited to have her friend Nori over to play. She picked out dress-up clothes and dolls to play with. She excitedly waited by the door for her friend to arrive. She jumped up and down when she saw her coming up the walk. Yet, from the moment Nori entered, Layla shrieked, "Noooo!" about whatever her friend approached. She followed her around and took toys out of her hand. She insisted she not touch her stuffed animals, train set, or play kitchen. Embarrassed and frustrated, her mother suggested they watch a short video. But even then, Layla demanded Nori sit in only one place. "What is going on with her?" her mother asked when she reported the incident. I noted that Layla, who normally was excited to have a friend over, had a high need for control. "Is anything new going on in her life?" I asked. "Any changes?" It turns out there were two big things. Layla had started wearing underpants just that week, with "no accidents so far," and her mother had been out of town for work. There usually is a reason that conflict reaches higher-than-normal levels. And when it does, rather than thinking your child will share and be nice, cut the playdate short. It is okay to send a child home, with apologies, when your child is having a hard time. Try again another day.

Parenting POV
"Is My Child Okay?"

In this culture of highly competitive preschools and the pressure to get into the right kindergarten, parents are understandably sensitive to how their children learn and if they are learning enough. Is my child gifted? Is he different? Can she keep up? These are routine questions I receive regularly. It is often in the form of concerns like: *She doesn't talk very much and I see other children her age talking so much more. He won't sit for long. She falls a lot. She won't participate in any toddler classes. He wants to do the same activity all day, every day.* It's important to keep in mind that in the toddler years, children's brains and bodies are on fire with growth. They are sponges, absorbing and responding to the stimuli around them. There are two important issues to keep in mind: each toddler develops in his own pattern and at his own pace, and even though they are all learning, that doesn't mean they are ready to absorb information and learn it in the same way that a seven-, ten-, or fifteen-year-old studies information, understands new concepts, and remembers facts. Toddlers are just beginning to lay the foundation for cognitive skills. That is why these years are so vital; they are foundational to lifelong learning. Instead of learning in the ways they will when they are older, toddlers are preoccupied with emotional changes and challenges, becoming physically more mobile, agile, and independent, making sense of the world around them, and gaining a grasp on their ability to impact their environment. These are all skills they need to have to succeed in school, family, and life. With today's pressures, it can be easy to lose sight of what matters at this age and keep in mind what children ages two to five should be doing and can be doing, and that there is no one learning or development trajectory. Children can be strong in one area and lacking in another. My oldest was highly verbal before he was two, but equally reticent in any new situation. Separation was not his strength, but grasp of language was. My middle child talked later but could boldly scale up jungle gyms that his older brother would not even try. There is a huge range of normal development.

I cannot think of a time in the past when it was as important as it is now to highlight the real ways that toddlers learn. Years of developmental psychology research and more recent neuroscience studies confirm that play is the essence of toddler learning and the foundation for lifelong success in one's educational and personal endeavors. As I noted earlier, major U.S. employers are speaking out about the lack of problem-solving, communication, creativity, and organizational skills they see in recent college graduates. The years from ages two to five provide a profoundly important time to guide your child onto a path to a love of learning and developing life skills necessary to succeed educationally and in life. But to do so, we have to look at the toddlers in the context of their development. What may be the way to set them up for success and a fulfilled life is not always obvious. If we offer them opportunities to explore, in dynamic and rich sensory environments, children will naturally take the lead of their own learning. They will explore, they will follow their curiosity, they will focus their attention and follow through. Adults are there to set up the environment, then sit back, observe, and provide guidance; this is what it means to follow the child's lead rather than setting an adult's agenda. As soon as parents or adults interfere by giving too much direction, too much structure, and academic-like activities that are outside the skills of this developmental age, kids will back off and turn away. That means turning away from learning.

Toddlers count on adults to provide them with structured, safe, and inviting environments for play. Once the environment (classroom, bedroom, playroom, backyard) is set up, the toddler has the freedom to decide what and how to play within it. This is where initiative, motivation, persistence, flexibility, problem solving, creativity, and innovation are incubated for the child. These are all skills that have been identified as necessary for future success. Thinking back to earlier chapters, recall that toddlers thrive on predictability and routines. That means repetitive play is the norm, and knowing where to find things and in what order helps them feel safe and supports their budding independence. A concerned mother reported to me that her two-and-a-half-year-old "will only play with his train. Every day. Pushing it around and around and around sometimes for over an hour." She was concerned that nothing good could come out of this. I asked who set up the track. "He does," she reported. At the mere age of two he had figured out how to make a track out of the pieces, how to pick the trains he wanted each time, and how to get the magnets together so the train could go. Did he get frustrated if the train fell apart? "Absolutely!" she noted. But he also recovered and went back to playing. He was doing new things every day, managing his frustration, deriving pleasure and learning, but he found comfort in the repetition of the same train on the same track, over and over.

Good early childhood classrooms have materials in the same place each day and a set routine that children can follow. At home, you can do something similar by keeping out a minimal number of toys and books (too many possibilities makes it harder to choose) and have shelves or bins for them, so your child knows where they are and can access them on his own (and help to put them away!). This is a way to support their growing independence and ability to make choices.

The incredible curiosity of the toddler and desire to know the world on their terms drives toddler play, the root of lifelong learning. They naturally play, indoors and out. Play is their context for learning. One is not separate from the other. Play allows them to figure out their newly discovered self, the world around them, their feelings and experiences as well as what goes together and comes apart. Figuring-it-all-out is the heart of toddler play. It becomes problem solving and sets up confidence in learning. And even though they may appear self-focused and selfish at times, what they are doing is learning through play. Learning in all areas, including how to get along with others. And these are the emotional, social, and cognitive skills that set the foundation for a positive attitude toward lifelong learning.

chapter nine

A Lab for Later

The Fifteen New Seeds for Success

Parenting is frontloaded. As parents, we put so much—love, thought, time, energy, worries, hopes—into our relationships and interactions with our children so that they can grow into the best people they can be and the person they are meant to be, which can be different from what we envision for any of our children. But who that person will be is far from clear at the ages of two to five, and it won't be known until much later. What this means is that we do whatever we think is best to raise them now to be successful in life—caring and kind, smart, well-behaved, motivated, resourceful, and resilient—later.

I have found that with these aspirations in mind, the key to parenting in every one of its dimensions is a *balance* between providing our children with comfort and love, and guidance, boundaries, and limits, while letting them try things on their own, take risks, make choices, venture out in the world, fall down, and get up again. It is not always clear to any of us where this exact balance is, and that is the core of the challenge parents face every day.

As you've read throughout this book, toddlers are at a vibrant, complex, and exciting stage of growth. Every ounce of their being is trying to figure out who they are, what the world is all about, and to be sure they can count on their parents (or caregivers) to be there for them, no matter what. This takes place in the context of a brain that is developing in leaps and bounds, with lots of fluctuation. Toddler brains are essentially works in progress. For this reason, toddlers' way of thinking, seeing the world, communicating, and expressing and handling emotions is wildly different from our own as adults. Thus seeing the world from your child's view can radically shift your understanding of their behavior and reactions—why they do what they do and how to handle it.

Remember, You're in Charge. It's Not About Control.

In this era of media, parents have access to a tremendous and at times overwhelming amount of information on how to raise their toddlers. A major category of toddler advice uses an approach that is top-down, parent-enforced control. This is misguided for many reasons, especially if your goal is long term: to raise children to become the best people they can be, who become independent and know how to handle life in all its ups and downs, care about others, who can make good choices and decisions and succeed in life. It is misguided for another reason: you are in control anyhow—simply by being the parent. There will be plenty of times it does not feel that way, or you may forget this principle, but it is true. In fact, your child counts on you to be the one in charge, to show them the way, to provide comfort and reassurance when life gets rough (which can be as simple as missing the final puzzle piece or bigger when they fall down and get hurt), to tell them when they've gone too far or far enough (limits) and to help them move out in the world. You are also responsible for your child's well-being.

But none of this implies forcing a child to act a certain way without considering who they are as individuals. In fact, try as you might, using control and force to get a toddler to behave or act in a certain way ignores his or her point of view. And in the end it will most likely backfire as they grow and develop.

A top-down control approach overlooks your child's needs and instead focuses on what you as a parent need or are wishing for in your child (which is often peace and quiet or avoiding being embarrassed by your child). Remember the harm of such approaches and of overlooking who your child is and their needs at this time. When you forget to interact with your child from his or her point of view, you risk causing shame to set in, just as they are developing their core sense of self. Most parents don't want their child's core sense of themselves as a person to be sprinkled with feeling ashamed of who they are and what they desire.

I also think of the control/top-down approach as one of "When the cat's away the mice will play." In other words, do you think your toddler will somehow magically know how to act when the "Enforcer" is not around? Probably not. Why would she? Paradoxically, attempts to force control on your child lead to increased—not reduced—control battles as well as the child's escalating desire to be freed from your control. Control battles will naturally occur anyhow as your child tries to figure out how much power she really has. That is where the testing of limits comes in. Instead, helping your child gain internal mechanisms of control, which reside within themselves (and which takes time, patience, nuance, and a good dose of humor), is the ultimate way for young children during this precious and important span of time to learn how they can manage their own desires, emotions, and impulses.

So if your goal is a well-adjusted child down the road, keep in mind that what you are laying down now for your child is a foundation to develop executive functions, the most important underlying skills for life success. Neuroscientists are now studying these functions and identifying where in the brain they reside, primarily in areas under development during these early years. These include the ability to self-regulate and handle emotions, think through problems and consequences, plan and make thoughtful decisions, adapt to change, and handle stressors, as discussed throughout this book. These are the indispensable skills for life success. You are also setting up your child's core sense of self, feelings of security, and confidence.

Margalit, at nearly three, was ecstatic over the first large snowfall. She'd run in her yard, pick up snow, feeling it on her mittens, and eating it, too. Her mother was disgusted. Snow is dirty! She repeatedly tried to stop her. "No eating the snow," she firmly demanded. We suggested she find clean snow on the bushes and let Margalit eat that or simply ignore the behavior. No way. Her mother threatened to take her inside early. She followed her around to stop her.

The next week, with more snow falling, we found pure and clean snow and put it in our water table. Toddlers love to play with snow indoors, no mittens on their hands, feeling the cold. Her caregiver gave our teachers strict instructions: "Do not let her eat that snow. Her parents will be upset." As the afternoon wore on, Margalit approached the table. We tried to dissuade her, to no avail. She was excited to feel the cold snow on her hands. Some toddlers might try to eat it, once and maybe twice. But out of twelve children at school that day, she was the only one who would not stop eating it. Enforcer away? Behavior escalates.

As I mentioned earlier, by first understanding where your child is developmentally and what he or she is experiencing in the here and now, you will come to understand the seemingly wacky and zany world they live in—it is truly not seen through the same colored glasses we adults wear. Nor has their brain developed to maturity yet, a point they will reach in twenty or more years. The world of young children is colored by and bathed in innocence and wonder, a focus on Me!, and a quest to satisfy desires immediately. ("Now. Now. Now!" is their motto.) So the first step a parent can take is to understand this. Not so you can indulge their every whim, far from that; but to have an idea of what they are experiencing. That does not mean giving in to every moment-to-moment desire. In fact, the opposite is true: by using these guidelines, adapted to your specific family situation and child, you will begin to help your child function in *spite* of his or her constant and changing desires and need for instant gratification. Understanding the context of their world and the world through toddler eyes (bizarre as that can appear to us as adults) helps frame their behavior and needs in ways more understandable to you or anyone taking care of them. And ways that let your child know she is understood. Once you get this, and truly accept and embrace it, you can and will figure out what to do, with less conflict, less angst, and more enjoyment with your child and family.

• A Lab for Later •

Parenting young children *is a lab for later.* By definition it is a long-term project where the outcome and benefits (who the child becomes) are most evident years later. Often parents get overly focused on the here and now and worry that if they don't jump in and stop a "bad behavior" immediately then they will be "setting a precedent." But what is precedent? I hear this often from parents: "If I let her do that now, then I am setting a precedent. I'll always have to let her do that." Worry, fear, and frustration follow on the parent's part.

As we've been seeing throughout this book, when parents get caught in their own fear and try to control their young children's behavior, they often unwittingly undermine their own authority and accentuate their child's lack of control over their own behavior. I guarantee you that if you view parenting as a power game, with you as the parent trying to assert control over your child, then you will have to keep upping the power to win. And the child, over time, will continue to battle, fighting back as he tries to show you with greater and greater force who he is, what he can do, what he needs from you. Or he will give up the battle altogether with feelings of resignation, right at the time when he is developing a sense of who he is. "I am a loser. I can't win. Why keep trying?" This is not what parents tell me they want their child to feel in life or in school—that they are the loser and that their desires must be wrong or bad and can be crushed.

If you want the battles to decrease and still have your child flourish in life, then you have to understand what the battle means *to your young child* and where it is coming from. Only then can you handle it differently and in a way that helps your child develop into the best person he can be. The young child is fighting to become her own person, different from the adolescent or another adult who has a stronger, more experienced sense of who they are. The young child's sense of self is in formation, supported by your reassuring presence, love, limits, and guidance.

So how does moving beyond control set the foundation for a future in which your child will know who she or he is and gain the skills needed to develop, learn, and grow, and in which you and your child will have a trusting, loving, empathic relationship? Parenting now sets the groundwork for later. It is the opportunity to help your child become the person you want them to be at that later time when they need you less, that older child or teen who becomes capable and caring, planful and persistent, able to handle life and reach out to others. What we do now is to help lay this path for our child to grow into that older child, teen, or adult who embodies these qualities.

Why is this so true? Like it or not, humans were not built in a linear fashion. It would be so easy if we were. If the process of development were linear, rational, and logical, there would be no need for parenting books or advice. We would all develop on the same linear path. But development is the antithesis of linear: it's circuitous, it's dynamic, it's interactive, and it always depends on context. As we saw earlier, it's not nature versus nurture: it's nature *and* nurture. And the intersection of the two can be quite complicated.

Instead of a linear progression, where one piece gets set into place followed by the next, like building blocks, the way we develop is much more in a pattern of two steps forward and one (or even three) steps back. Just as your three-year-old masters sleeping in his big-boy bed, he has toileting accidents for the first time in months. Similarly, when your four-year-old finally feels comfortable at school and skips off without any problems, she wakes crying that night. As one father said, "I wished so much that he would feel better at school and not cry when I took him. It just made me feel so bad. Who knew what I was wishing for? He runs in happy now but is demanding so much more at home. Everything has to be his way!" This too will even out, but one area of development rubs against another.

I often find that when parents come to see me with more general concerns, such as "she is just out of sorts—throwing tantrums, overly sensitive to other people, and refusing to eat foods she used to eat," it often means the child is on the verge of a big developmental shift. I imagine that the brain is reorganizing for a developmental leap forward, and before it does, it gets shaken up, kind of like a snow globe when you shake it. And then, soon after, just as the "snow" in the snow globe settles back down and the globe is clear again, the child settles back in with a bigger vocabulary, or suddenly increased imaginary play capacities or another new physical skill. Again, the developmental change is not one step and then another; it is closer to a shake-up followed by a settling in. This is because the groundwork for any new skill is being laid, in ways big and small, every day, even though we may not be aware of it. And suddenly the pieces come together and click. He's reading! She can ride a bike! He can sit through the story time! But it certainly feels hard when you are right in the throes of the shake-up and unsure of where it will land. It can be hard for your child, too.

The very interactive nature of child development is what makes it essential that parents cue in to their child and stay involved. Not by controlling and demanding, nor by making your child's life a free-for-all. Rather, when you are present and aware, and tap into your child's unique combination of very universal, normal needs and their own individual ways of moving in the world, while you provide love, support, and guidance, then the fits and starts that challenge us as parents are just that—reflections of their growth.

In fact, there are ways to provide a healthy foundation for your child that include structure and boundaries, without battling all the time and destroying your young child's sense of self. At times, the balance of who is setting the limits and structure may feel tipped toward the child, especially when you have a demanding and hard-to-satisfy toddler living with you (I call this the "benign dictator" stage). But in reality, the balance really starts in your favor, the parent. And that is something you need to keep in mind. Our children count on us to know we are in charge. That is the only way they feel safe, when the scale is tipped toward the parents as the providers, guiders, and comforters!

That is what this entire book has been about: understanding how to guide your child in the best way, so they can become their best possible self. Establishing clear boundaries, regular routines, and realistic limits are a parent's best set of tools for managing children's behavior in a supportive way, in a way that enables the child to practice and learn to handle his or her own behavior, feelings, and desires, all within the context of the brain's complex and rapid growth during these toddler years.

What follows then are what I call my Fifteen *New* Seeds for Success, which I've mentioned throughout the book in ways explicit and subtle. I list them here because I believe now you will truly appreciate how they can work for you, your children, and your family.

• The Fifteen *New* Seeds for Success •

1. **Go to where the child (toddler) is.** In order to best support our toddlers, we have to first understand where they are developmentally and what they are experiencing. That provides the context for understanding the sometimes bizarre and seemingly irrational world they live in. It is a view of the world far from what we see out of our adult eyes. Their world is driven by an insatiable curiosity, a desire to figure things out on their own terms, and a startling need for immediate gratification without a sense of time. This does not mean giving in to their every desire. In fact, it is just the opposite that children need in order to succeed. They need you, the parent, to keep them safe within all these desires by providing a place to safely explore, figure out the world, and be curious. So understanding the context of their world helps frame their behavior and needs in ways more understandable to the adult. Ask yourself questions like, What is my child experiencing? What does this look like to him? Feel like to her? Once you get this, even if it seems bizarre, you can figure out what to do. Remember the child who was afraid to go with his parents on a trip because he would "get small and disappear" like planes do? Knowing this view allowed the parent to provide comfort and address his fears, and the boy stopped having tantrums.
2. **Have humor. Laugh a lot.** Humor and laughter make for serious parenting. I say this now with authority since the earliest years of my own children's lives are now behind me. These early years do go by fast even

if it does not feel this way. I had more than a decade of young childhood in my home. It was exhausting. It was exhilarating. It was pleasurable. It was challenging. But it is now done. Humor not only helps you get through those tough moments, or days or weeks; it also makes being a parent more enjoyable. How much can you let go, kick back, and laugh? It will be a lot more fun (and easier) that way. And your children will enjoy it more, too. One way or the other, you have to get through it. And you will.

Humor helps.

3. **Keep things the same, so your child can learn how to deal with change and adapt.** The importance and need for routines cannot be underestimated. Routines and regularity develop flexibility and resilience. If you want your child to become flexible over time, then change nothing, or as little as you can. It sounds contradictory, but it's true.

   The more structure and routines, the freer the child. But not with rigidity. It is one of the many paradoxes of being a parent, that you have to set basic routines and yet also have the flexibility to move with the moment. This is what breeds flexibility in the child. Any task that is a daily happening will go smoother and help your child on the road to independence if it is structured around a routine. That includes mealtimes, bedtime, getting dressed, brushing teeth, bath, and getting out the door. These daily routines, where the child can count on things staying the same, will also prepare your child for handling change and transitions.

4. **Let them lean on you.** This is not overcoddling. This is about recognizing that the more toddlers move

away and go out to explore, the more they need you. Dependence now leads to independence later. Babying the child now, letting them need you and being available to respond to those needs, leads to independence later. They learn they can count on you no matter how big they grow or how far out in the world they go. **You are their rock.** But it is all about balance, letting them go, but also supporting them. A fine line, I know, but an important one to wrestle with and work out. The child who is led all the time (that is, by the parent) can never learn to lead, to take initiative, or to do for themselves. Being led too much or being micromanaged (as parents can do—especially with our firstborns!) creates more rather than less dependence. A child learns to make decisions and do things for themselves by participating and practicing, making mistakes and trying again.

5. **Let siblings work it out on their own.** Siblings fight. The more they hate, the more they love. I call sibling relationships the lab for life. Sibling love is rooted in the history they share, the growing up together, and the sharing of parents. Sibling jealousy (or hate) is based in these same three points. So what that means is that siblings are naturals for love but also naturals for jealousy. They are automatically put in a position of having to share the parent(s). Who really wants to do that?! It means sharing their safe base, their rock, the person they count on the most. The reason sibling relationships are a lab for life is that siblings have a very special and loving bond—if the parents stay out of their relationships. And within this bond they learn to work out their

place in the family and resolve conflict between each other. They fight. They play. They look out for each other. One moment they are fighting, screaming, and rolling around. Just as you think you had better go prevent some accident from happening, they are laughing and playing. It can change in a moment. Ever watch puppies pounce and play and nip at each other? Sometimes it looks quite vicious, then suddenly they run off, lie down, snuggle, and go to sleep together. Siblings are like puppies. You have to leave them be, let them have their love/hate relationship, and not intervene in their battles, because a parent can never be the impartial judge. When you intervene, you take sides, and that undermines their special bond. Expressing the jealousy and conflict between them is what frees up the love side, even if it is hard as parents to watch them fight. Ultimately they have each other for life, no matter how different they may be. As the Toddler Center founder Pat Shimm says, "It should be parents on one side and kids on the other side. Then they can be best friends for life." Let them be their own friends in all the good and hard ways!

6. **Let go of perfection.** Perfect is a fantasy. Life is messy. Let them (and yourself) make mistakes. Mistakes, mischief, and errors make up the perfect human child. Humanity is not about perfection. Child development is not about perfection. Growing up is not about perfection. And there is no such thing as a perfect parent. Be a good enough parent. Growing and developing is about foibles, slip-ups, and vulnerabilities, falling down, and making

mistakes. A child cannot move forward unless they make mistakes, through trial and error. Children need to be able to take risks in order to test themselves and move ahead. Children have to be allowed to try on their own, fall down, make mistakes, then try again—from learning to walk to learning to read to learning how to be friends to learning how to act at grandma and grandpa's house. Control is an attempt to override their ever making a mistake—to make them do it a certain way. But we all learn best when we can figure it out ourselves, and that includes errors and blunders along the way. Children *learn* from their mistakes. Think of it this way: the baseball Hall of Famer Reggie Jackson, whose October home runs carried his team to several World Series victories, also holds the record for most major-league strikeouts, with 2,597. Victory comes through striking out.

7. **Hands-off, not hands-on parenting.** What does hands-off mean when it comes to parenting? How do you do it, especially in this hovering environment where often parents are told to monitor their child's every move? Here's the rub: We render our children helpless when all is done for them—when they are micromanaged. When we hover, we make our children feel insecure, not secure. Instead of showing them we trust them, we inadvertently signal that we don't believe in their capabilities. This is true when we micromanage their schedules and criticize how they do things. They may struggle to get a shoe on, and you likely know an easier and faster way, but saying "This is the *right* way to do it" gives

your child self-doubt ("I don't know how to do it right"), leads them to second-guess themselves, and makes the child mistrust his own judgment. When we kindly remind our children that there is only one right way to do it, the child hears "I am doing it wrong. I can't do it. I don't know how." She doubts herself and feels ashamed of her attempts.

But hands-off is not a free-for-all, either. This is where balance comes in. Our children need our guidance and limits. Hold the shoe so she can figure out how to get it on. Comfort him when frustration sets in after many tries at something new. The idea is to give our children space to try, and to try again, and to reassure and comfort them when the going gets tough. But not to criticize and diminish their attempts—successful or not.

8. **Set limits and boundaries.** Limits and boundaries are the frame for freedom and creativity. Children learn freedom only when clear and reasonable limits are set. Otherwise, they don't feel safe; they feel out of control. Children feel taken care of when they know when to stop because you have told them what the limit is. Two to five is an age of testing out who they are and their level of power. It is too scary to think their power is unlimited. They want to know you will keep them safe (even if they battle you!). The world they are exploring during these years is a big place. There is much to learn, much to see, and so much to figure out, from learning about emotions, to figuring out how to get their needs met; from learning to have and make friends to figuring out how things work; from testing out their power to figuring

out what they like and dislike. So much is going on and they cannot do it solely on their own. Children count on parents to set up limits and guidelines, to show them when to stop and let them know we will keep them safe. The feeling that they are not on their own, that we are setting limits, gives them security and feelings of comfort. When parents set reasonable limits ("At dinnertime, we sit to eat; when you run around, dinner is done." "You can throw the ball in this basket, but not at other people.") children are freed up to explore and figure it all out. Limits and boundaries also guide them toward a more socialized way of being in the world. I like to say that the limits and boundaries we set up and reinforce save them from themselves. Deep inside, they want to know that we will not let them go too far.

9. **Let the children play.** By themselves, with each other, and without adult interference. Set up a safe environment and the children naturally will play, indoors or out. Play is learning and learning is play, if we let our children play on their own terms and make decisions about what and how they want to play. That is the mode of young children. Adults provide support and guidance but the play is about the children. There is no such thing as "just playing" for a toddler. Play is their stage for developing. Through play they learn in all areas of development—about who they are, how the world works, how to make decisions and figure things out, how to handle emotions and get along with others, how to think and problem-solve; they learn the foundations of number sense and of reading, of colors and shapes,

rhythms and patterns. But playing at these ages goes even far beyond what they learn right now. It lays the tracks for their lifelong learning. Play establishes a love of learning, an ability to try new things, to take chances, make mistakes and try again, make changes, adapt, invent, create, and troubleshoot. This is the root of the most important skills the brain is developing—executive function skills that are needed for academic and lifelong success.

10. **Stop praising your child.** *Praise defeats. Let them have and enjoy their own success.* If you want a motivated and persistent child who feels good about themselves and what they can do, who owns their accomplishments *and* their mistakes, then don't cheer for them at each turn, move, or accomplishment. Cheering them on knocks them down. It is another way of controlling your child, who is well tuned in to what you expect of them. Alfie Kohn calls praise "sugarcoated control." I couldn't agree more. The message to the toddler: *I am happy for you when you do it this way, my way. So you had better do it my way.* It is yet another way of controlling their behavior just as they are bursting to figure out what they can do and how the world works. Control, even in a seemingly sweet package of praise, backfires. It works against your child figuring out who they are and what they can do. Instead, they become focused on *what can I do to please mommy or daddy or the teacher?*

    You may be thinking, *But if I don't praise, how will she ever know how to act? Where does feeling good come from if not from being praised?* Take a step back and think about this. See if you can remember a time as a child where you had an "A-ha!" moment, where you figured something out on your own. Or a time when you worked really hard to fix something or reach a goal or learn something new. Do you remember how you felt inside? Did you have a sense of satisfaction? Of feeling good about yourself? Maybe even feeling empowered? It is just that feeling from deep inside that feels so good. It spurs children on to *want* to try again, try more, to *want* to figure things out, to *want* to explore and learn or do it again. The motivation resides within them and they carry it to new settings. But if the reward comes from adults who praise or give gold stickers, the child is left feeling they may have made you happy, but it is not about them, it is about you. And in a new setting, they will look for the person they need to please, rather than feeling motivated for themselves.

I once wrote a long poem in third grade about the color green and when I finished it I remember the thrill. I reread it and thought, *Wow! I am a poet. A real poet!* No grade. No teacher feedback. Just an inner feeling of excitement and satisfaction of doing something I had never done before. I felt good about it and more confident in my ability to try new things.

Praise is another way to control, to get our children to do what we want them to do. And children know that. It takes the achievement away from the child and says "You are a good child; you did this for Mommy, for Daddy, not for yourself." It is conditional. And conditional means that they feel loved when they make you happy, but not otherwise. It places self-doubt at the center of who they are. I know most parents don't want that for their child. Does that mean you can't enjoy your child? Hardly. Smile with them as they smile. Hug them when they come running to you with glee after learning a new skill at the playground. Then you are not taking away their achievement, you are there with them, following their lead and celebrating a shared joy and accomplishment.

11. **Let them be bored.** Boredom can be *good* for children. Give them lots of unstructured time. In an era of technology and toddler classes, when toddlers can be taking classes in gymnastics, violin, soccer, Italian, cooking, and art, all in a week, when their days can be scheduled from morning to evening, which means they are following the directions of adults, I wonder when they have time to wonder. To look around. To nurture their natural curiosity. To figure out who they are and what they like, on their own terms. To be bored. Yes, bored. That old-fashioned concept. But in fact, boredom may not be what you think it is. Sitting and staring into space? We once called it daydreaming. And out of daydreaming come ideas and vision, dreams and imagination, and maybe even relaxation. So "doing nothing" may not really be that. In fact, much can go on when a child is *bored,* if bored is truly what is happening. Boredom or "doing nothing" can be a pause, a time to sit back, to regroup, to collect one's thoughts, to reflect, to look around and observe, or simply to rest and

clear the mind. All are needed in order to reengage. To plan and be thoughtful. To let new information sink in and get absorbed. To make decisions. Boredom can be a time to think about what to do next, which allows children to develop initiative and agency. They can figure out what to do and how to do it on the road to those motivating feelings of "I can do it!"

Boredom can also be a warning if it means your child is so overscheduled and directed in activities and play that when left to their own initiative, they are completely stuck. They can't make a decision about what to do, even with your guidance. Too much instruction and being led and directed can turn to this kind of "boredom," a signal that they need more down time.

But unstructured time is not the same as boredom. Unstructured time means giving children the space to play on their own, without adult direction. They need a lot of it at these ages. This is where the magical and wondrous world of toddler play unfolds, the play I discussed earlier that is their arena for life, for exploration, and for learning. It is where most toddler learning takes place, so give them plenty of space and time for it.

12. **Cut down on the rules.** The more rules, the more battle. So what are structure and routine without lots of rules? The balance between structure and routine and not micromanaging can seem hard at first. How do you do one without the other? I think of it this way: The structure we provide our children through routines and how we set up their environ-

ment is the big picture—the outline of the path, a road map. They need a good road map. Rather than telling them exactly how to do something step by step, we set up a space for them—from home to schoolroom to playgrounds to playspaces—and give them limits and guidelines so they can choose within these guidelines how to navigate or figure it out.

A wonderful early childhood provider I know who grew up in Eastern Europe under a dictatorial government describes it this way: "When I was growing up, the adult would give a child a tricycle. They would draw a straight line and show the child how to pedal it from point A to point B. And the child would do just that. They called it learning. But now I know that is not how to do it. Instead, you give a child a tricycle. Then create a safe backyard space, with hedges or a fence around the outside, a safe space with lots of room to ride. Then you let the child go. The child figures out how to ride it and makes their own path for riding."

That is what I mean by structure rather than strict rules. A road map, a safe space with boundaries to move in. Sitting at a table for dinner and talking about the day is a road map for how to "do" a meal with other people. Reading books before bedtime gives a road map of how to finish the day and wind down for bedtime. Toddlers need us to guide them if our goal is to help children become more independent over time. And that is what structure does. It gives the child the ability to *choose* how to walk or run or pedal on the roadway—a straight line, back and forth, touching the edge, and so on.

And they all get to the end of the road, in their unique style. Lots of rules will set up lots of battles at this age. Paradoxically, at certain times, a toddler breaking the rules can be a sign of healthy development.

13. **Let them be selfish so they can become generous later.** Sharing comes later. This may be the hardest one to grasp. The idea that being selfish can lead to generosity goes against everything we value as adults. We all want to raise children who are kind and generous to others, but also can take care of themselves. So before a child can take notice of another's needs and be kind and giving, they have to satisfy the first step—to develop their own sense of self and feel that they are taken care of. This is not a momentary feeling of being taken care of. It is a feeling that develops, over time, deep inside. When it is firmly in place, after age two or three, they start to be generous to others. Feeling taken care of means feeling they have *all* they need. It is complicated. First a sense of self as their own person has to develop, then a sense of ownership and that their needs are fulfilled. Only after this is firmly set can the ability emerge to look out for others, to be empathic and share.

The foundation for sharing is a true paradox. It is about establishing a sense of *me, mine and my needs being met first.* Part of being Me is having everything I need—that includes comfort and emotional fulfillment as well as holding on to whatever objects are deemed "mine." By forcing or persuading children to share before they are ready, we ask them to give up a piece of what they need, because at two and three, that is what it feels like. Allowing them to hold on to what they need at these ages allows them to let go later and be compassionate. Soon (around three and a half) they want other children to be part of their life, and when their needs have been fulfilled, they start to see that other children have needs and desires, too. Other children are also fun to play with! The desire to make friends and play together is when the motivation to share begins. They want to have friends; they want to be liked. And sharing is part of that world. But not until after those seemingly selfish "me, mine" needs are met.

14. **Accept your children for who they are.** *Even the parts you don't like.* Don't shame your child. Everybody's good. Everybody's bad. That's part of being a kid (or adult!). Toddlers are just getting to know themselves. They are figuring out who they are. They are experiencing a wider range of emotions than they did as infants. As they figure out who they are, they have a *lot* of needs (for attention; or desires to fill) and are coming up against limits. As adults we want our children to become more socialized, and to get there we set up limits (as you should!). At the same time, toddlers begin to recognize their own limitations as they muddle through new experiences. In response to these inner and outer limits, they have bad thoughts (*I am mad at Daddy for not letting me climb on Grandma's white couch*!). They grapple with negative feelings like anger and frustration. They do bad things (throw, hit, not listen, push the limits). Part of figuring out who they are is making mistakes and not always doing what the adults expect of them. They are test-

ing to see how much power they have and looking for control in a world of adventure and exploration that can feel overwhelming. This all can lead to clashes with mommy and daddy—the people they love and count on most.

What it comes to for your child is learning to accept that *sometimes I am good and sometimes I am bad*. That is human. But when we expect our children, including our naturally compliant ones, to be good all (or most) of the time, we give them the message that the "bad" parts (thoughts, feelings, actions) of who they are are unacceptable to us. And that is scary to them. It floods them with shame, which blocks healthy development. Remember, they are just now figuring out who they are, and these "bad" parts are still part of them. Instead, let your child know that you love her for all she is—good and bad. Even if you stop her from doing an unsocialized action (kicking people, throwing food, running too far in a crowd), you still love her. Even when you say "no" to another cookie and he screams, you still love him. Your child learns that part of being a kid is doing things and having thoughts and feelings both bad and good, yet you remain her mommy (or daddy) who loves her through it all!

15. **Help them handle the negative.** *Remember, it's not your job to make them happy.* Most parents say they want their children to be happy. They want their child to grow up to be a kind and productive person who is *happy.* The misnomer is thinking that we can make our child be happy, that if we fill their every need then they will be happy. Sometimes

parents try to cater to their child's every whim, only to find it is not enough. Their child still is not happy. The truth is this: *No parent can make his or her child happy all the time.* Children know how to be happy. What they are not so good at is handling the hard times. This is where you, the parent, come in. Want happiness? Our job is to set them up to handle life more and more on their own, and to gradually let go. At the center of this is helping them deal with life's hurdles. How do you do that? By supporting them to handle negatives in life—negative feelings, disappointments, rejections, errors, and setbacks. That is the biggest gift you can give your child, *to equip them to handle the negative.* From there emerges happiness. Really. Because if your child feels certain that she can handle life, she is freed up to be content and happy.

In life, there will always be disappointments (when a best friend doesn't want to play or there is no more blue Play-Doh). There will always be negative feelings to understand, express, and manage—sadness, anger, fear, worry. There will always be bossy people and bullies (the child who insists, "You can't play!"). If we help our children handle life's so-called adversities, then they can go out and handle themselves even when there are hurdles. With our support, they develop the feeling that they are still okay, even when things don't go their way, even when life doesn't feel good, even when mommy says no. They may not like it, but they can handle it. The catch is that a child can only have this competence if we let them face the tough times—whatever they are—and help them through. After the frustration, yelling, and stomping of feet because he could not get the final Lego piece to fit into his just-made building, your child settles down with a big hug from you. His lesson? *It doesn't feel good, but Mommy is still here to comfort me, and I am okay. I got through it and now I can try again when I am ready.* That is what I mean by helping your child through the negative.

When children can deal with negative feelings in themselves, they will see them in others and reach out to help. When they can handle the negatives, they will have the strength to get back up when they fall down, to recover from being upset, and to build again when the tower they worked so hard to make collapses. Limits set by adults or by their inexperience will get in their way and so will other people who are not so kind or don't understand what they need. You can help your child learn to handle these situations and to feel that they are still okay. Then they can learn to problem-solve, to not be overwhelmed by adversity. When we help our children handle these frustrations and stressors in life, we are preparing them for life, for happiness and for generosity. Children who can navigate through the hurdles (and there will always be some) become resilient, persistent, and confident that "I can handle it!" It opens them up to other people. But they don't learn this on their own; they learn it when we guide and comfort them and help them navigate the hurdles. Handling life in all its ups and downs is what puts them on the path toward happiness and fulfillment.

A Final Note to Take with You

Just as toddlers struggle to figure out who they are, gain independence, and still know that they are loved by you and can count on you through thick and thin, parents struggle, too. Parenting young children is simply hard work. We put our all into it, but in return, what comes back to us day to day is not always pleasant, or easy, or even nice. Parenting, especially of children at these young ages (and perhaps again at adolescence), is not about getting validation and thank-yous or overt appreciation from our children. Sure, they say thank you at certain times, but our children's role is not to make us happy. It is not to make us feel good. We put our all into them because we love them, and our hope is that one day they will turn out to be those people we envision them to be. Keep that long-term goal in mind as you move through the ups and downs, joyful and not so joyful moments of being a parent of young children. It is hard, because often this involves putting our own expectations aside in order to allow our children to become who they are meant to be, which can be quite different from who we had envisioned.

When we step aside but still provide support, our children can grow and blossom, with us out of their way yet still close by. Without them feeling ashamed of who they are, what they feel, or how they see the world—whether it is similar to how we see it or different.

Parenting is hard for other reasons, too. It is nonstop. We can't simply bow out and then return when we feel ready. Our children, especially at this pivotal toddler period, count on us to be there for them. We are their constant. We are their security. We are their safety in a big and unpredictable world. If we go to work, they count on us to come home to them. If we say we will pick them up at school, they count on us to do so. A business trip or weekend away with a spouse or partner? They count on us to return, just as we said we would. Simply put, they rely on us to be their rock and stability, to pick them up when they fall down and to still love them even when they have done things well beyond our liking or outside of our wildest imagination. Parenting is not an occasional role—it is an always role. To be there, sitting back, while being available, letting them go, yet being at the ready for comfort, not interfering but not forgetting what they need. It is likely the hardest role you will ever have, and at the same time, the most pleasurable and deeply meaningful one as well.

Even with all the joys and pleasures, the smiles and accomplishments and surprises that being a parent of a young child brings (and there are many!), parenting is rarely logical or clear. Figuring out how to provide that comfort and reassurance your child craves while letting them grow, go, move further out in the world and explore, is a tricky line to toe. The one thing I know parents have in common is a desire to raise their children as best they can, so they can become the best person they can be. But the route to that outcome is frequently not easy to decipher, and the journey is filled with bumps and pitfalls that you likely never knew would occur. Your individual child's style and ways in the world call for a tailoring of your approach to what it is they need, but it's not always easy to know just what that is.

So, along the way mistakes will happen; you'll let your child down, overlook their need of the moment, especially as they negotiate their pull for independence and need for more space. In these moments, when we've failed to know what our children need, because maybe it is just impossible to know at that moment—or we've simply done the wrong parenting thing—we have to be lighter on ourselves, to remember that being a parent is hard, relationships are complicated and messy, and life with a toddler is not simple, yet we can always go back and repair. We can say we're sorry and reconnect with our child. We can hug them and let them know we still love them. No parent is perfect. And children are forgiving.

When we keep long-term goals in mind, remembering that the toddler years are a lab for later, the immediate interactions take on a different meaning. It is the collective experience over time that helps your child internalize those all-important life skills and lessons: the ability to relate and have compassion as well as to feel competent and handle life; the ability to think through situations and decide on which path to take; the ability to feel and handle emotions, then move on and reengage; the ability to try again and be passionate about what they do; the ability to look out for others and see their needs, even when it means putting their own needs aside. All of this can and does develop, but it takes time. No single interaction, as long as it is in the context of a caring and loving relationship, makes the child who they are. So you will blunder and fail them, and the repair can happen, too. Keep your humor. Be sure to laugh at yourself and together with your child. It helps a lot.

And yet, as the story has been told in the chapters of this book, the ages from two to five are crucial for your child's long-term healthy development and success—for laying the foundation of who they will become over time. The drives to separate and become their own person are intense and bring them to new crossroads and emotional experiences. They are trying to be apart from you yet intimately connected, a fragile and complicated dance fraught with pitfalls.

The brain is developing in leaps and bounds, evident in the incredible growth we see in children from month to month and year to year. Yet growth also means stumbles and steps back—sometimes way back—and as parents, we need to remember this. As children grow up, they also need repeated reminders that they are still your baby. You are always their parent, even when they get big. Moving to a big bed, learning to ride a tricycle or scooter or two-wheeler, giving up a pacifier, using the toilet, going to school, dressing themselves, meeting new friends—these are all milestones and signs of growth. The funny thing about growing up is this: With every sign of growth, something is given up or lost. Another step toward independence and being big means one step further away from the former baby, or earlier toddler. All of this calls for reassurance that mommy and daddy will still take care of the child and be there when she needs us. Even when she gets big!

These steps forward can be just as tricky for parents. We may wish for them to outgrow a stage—to not scream their every need, to sleep through the night, move out of their crib, stop whining or throwing tantrums, or to dress themselves. And yet when they do succeed, we may miss the little one who did these baby things. We have to be aware of our inner experience and mixed feelings, too. That is what allows us to provide our kids with the support they need.

The key to being that good-enough parent that we all desire to be is to know yourself, to be open to change, and to be forgiving. Also consider what your ideas about being a parent are and where they come from. When you are too hard on yourself—every parent lets their child down, every parent makes mistakes—ask yourself if your expectations are reasonable. Are you too hard on yourself? Why? Whose voice do you hear whispering in your ear telling you that you are not good enough? Let yourself be human, which means doing it well sometimes and not well, too. If you can accept the imperfections in yourself, especially as a parent, it will help you accept the good and bad in your child as well and the bumpy roads they and you will travel together.

Our job as parents is to let our toddlers grow up, and that means letting go of our babies. Usually we want them to grow up but we still desire for them to need us. I can assure you of this: When we give them the space to move out into the world, to grow and try out life, to make mistakes on their way to figuring it all out, they do come back. Because they need us. They need us as a home base for support and acceptance and comfort. They need us in new ways as they grow. What they take from the toddler years, what they build deep inside their burgeoning inner selves and encode in their developing toddler brain, is a sense that we are there for them, that we will accept them for who they are, that mommy and daddy are home base. But we need to toe that line between giving them a road map of structure and limits and letting them be who they are, while we stay on the sidelines for comfort and care. Then our toddlers will have the strength to develop and grow into who they are meant to be.

Acknowledgments

This book has been years in coming, both in my thinking and in the encouragement and prodding of numerous friends, colleagues, and parents. You no longer need to ask, "When are you going to write that book?!" Your support, guidance, eyes, and ears all contributed to making it happen, each in your own way. There are many people behind this book, and I thank all of you.

The incredible and dynamic writing and book team: I must begin with Billie Fitzpatrick, writing partner extraordinaire. From our first meeting, you "got" what this book was meant to be. Your skills at listening, organizing, writing, editing, are unparalled. Through *all* the changes, your steadiness and calm kept me focused and afloat. I am so grateful. Two amazing book agents: Yfat Reiss Gendell, whose energy, insight, support, and razor-sharp vision never wane; Hannah Brown Gordon, it started with you. I'm so glad you reached out to ask if I wanted to write a book. And the entire Foundry team, including Erica Walker, Kirsten Neuhaus, Sara DeNobrega, and Emily Morton. I am just as fortunate on the publishing side: the Touchstone

Group—my editor, Michelle Howry, who believed in this book from the start; her assistant, Brendan Culliton; Touchstone's publisher, Stacy Creamer; associate publisher David Falk and his entire marketing team; Touchstone's editorial director, Sally Kim; Shida Carr and Touchstone's publicity team, and the Simon & Schuster sales team—especially those sales team toddler parents who personally connected to the book's message and made it their mission to share it and get it to the readers.

Friends reviewed drafts and gave feedback, and provided sustaining cheers and encouragement. My longtime friends who parent alongside me and keep my humor going at low parenting moments, you are always close by: Andrea Carmosino and Sheila Ponte; Laura Bennett Murphy, who also read and gave spot-on feedback. Friends in work and life, with this book and more: Lesley Sharp and Lisa Tiersten. Marci Klein, for your love and encouragement. Nim Tottenham, who willingly responded to repeated inquiries about the brain. Michele Berdy and Ilene Green for their insights, support, and encouragement. Yvonne Smith, whose work with and respect for children inspire me.

Sarah Jessica Parker, your generosity and willingness to be part of the book, and your support, advice, and belief in these ideas, mean a lot to me.

Mentors who remain friends shaped my understanding of children. Jane Kessler taught me to listen to what children are saying, to see them for who they are and respect that each moves in her own way. Sam Meisels, whose passion and advocacy for children inspire me as much now as they did thirty years ago; Martha Putallaz, who taught me how to step back and observe children without bias.

No working mom, even with a supportive family, can do it all on her own. Three wonderful women have provided warm, loving care to our children: Ildiko Nakaji, Thelma Merette, and Natacha Felix. You exemplify why every relationship matters.

The Barnard College Toddler Center staff, who contribute to making the Toddler Center the special place it is: Elizabeth Elsass keeps the daily running smooth, even in my absence; Karina Trujillo-Sanchez and Tricia Hanley lead our extraordinary toddler classroom; Nora Koutruba, who helped track down articles and books often at a moment's notice; and Rachel Flax, who is always willing to pitch in.

The Toddler Center parents: Your generosity in sharing your children and being part of our center inspires me year after year as I get to see the world through your unique toddlers' eyes. All of you teach me about the complexity of being a parent.

I am grateful to have my closest colleague, Pat Shimm, also as my close friend. You have encouraged me for twenty years without fail and pushed me out of my comfort zone. Your vision, openness, honesty, love, and passion for toddlers motivate me; your voice is intricately woven into this book.

My family continually shows me how relationships make us who we are: my brothers, Joe and Sam Klein, prove that sibling fighting-and-laughter during childhood becomes a deep bond as adults. My parents gave me a strong base: Nancy Klein, my model for how to do work and parenting, never doubted I'd complete this book; Bob Klein walks steadfast beside me in life, on strolls and on long walks.

My children, Elam, Aaron, and Jesse: You have taught me there are ups and downs, but if I can let go, take a deep breath, and (try to) see it from your view, then we all end up laughing. You are my greatest joy! Kenny, you helped me soar with this one. Not only do you keep us well fed, but your support for me on this enormous project has been constant. I love you.

References

Ainsworth, M. D. S., Bell, S. M., & Stayton, D. J. (1971). Individual differences in the strange situation behavior of one-year-olds. In H. R. Schaffer (Ed.), *The origins of human social relations*. (15–71). New York: Academic Press.

Assor, A., & Roth, G. (2010). Parental conditional regard as a predictor of deficiencies in young children's capacities to respond to sad feelings. *Infant and Child Development, 19*, 465–477.

Barry, R. A. & Kochanska, G. (2010). A longitudinal investigation of affective environment in families with young children: From infancy to early school age. *Emotion, 10*, 237–249.

Berger, R. H., Miller, A. L., Seifer, R., Cares, S. R., & LeBourgeois, M. K. (2012). Acute sleep restriction effects on emotion responses in 30- to 36-month-old children. *Journal of Sleep Research, 21*, 235–246.

Bernier, A., Carlson, S., Deschênes, M., & Matte-Gagné, C. (2012). Social factors in the development of early executive functioning: A closer look at the caregiving environment. *Developmental Science, 15,* 12–24.

Blair, C. (2002). School readiness: Integrating cognition and emotion in a neurobiological conceptualization of children's functioning at school entry. *American Psychologist 57,* 111–27.

Blair, C. & Diamond, A. (2008). Biological processes in prevention and intervention: The promotion of self-regulation as a means of preventing school failure. *Developmental Psychopathology, 20(3),* 899–911.

Bodrova, E., & Leong, D. L. (2007). *Tools of the mind: The Vygotskian approach to early childhood education.* Upper Saddle River: Merrill/Prentice Hall.

Bonawitz, E., Shafto, P. Hyowon, G., Goodman, N., Spelke, E., & Schulz, L. (2011). The double-edged sword of pedagogy: Instruction limits spontaneous exploration and discovery. *Cognition, 120,* 322–330.

Bronson, M. B. (2000). *Self-regulation in early childhood: Nature and nurture.* New York: Guilford.

Bowlby J. (1988). *A secure base: Parent-child attachment and healthy human development.* London: Routledge.

Center on the Developing Child at Harvard University (2011). *Building the brain's "air traffic control" system: How early experiences shape the development of executive function: Working Paper No. 11.* http://www.developing child.harvard.edu

Center on the Developing Child at Harvard University (2010). *The foundations of lifelong health are built in early childhood.* http://www.developingchild.harvard.edu.

Center on the Developing Child at Harvard University (2004). *Children's emotional development is built into the architecture of their brains: Working Paper No. 2.* http://www.developingchild.harvard.edu.

Derryberry, D., & Reed, M. (1996). Regulatory processes and the development of cognitive representations. *Development and Psychopathology, 8,* 215–34.

Diamond, A. (2013). Executive functions. *Annual Review of Psychology, 64,* 135–168.

Dunn, J. (2004). *Children's friendships: The beginnings of intimacy.* Oxford: Blackwell.

Elkind, D. (2007). *The power of play.* New York: Da Capo.

Fein, G. (1981). Pretend play in childhood: An integrative review. *Child Development, 52,* 1095–1118.

Galinsky, E. (2010). *Mind in the making: The seven essential life skills every child needs.* NAEYC special ed. New York: HarperCollins.

Ginsburg, K. R. (2007). The importance of play in promoting healthy child development and maintaining strong parent-child bonds. *Pediatrics, 119,* 187–191.

Gray, J. (2004). Integration of emotion and cognitive control. *Current Directions in Psychological Science, 13,* 46–48.

Gunnar, M. R. (2007). The neurobiology of stress and development. *Annual Review of Psychology, 58,* 145–173.

Gunnar, M. R., Broderson, L., Nachimas, M., Buss, K., & Rigatuso, R. (1996). Stress reactivity and attachment security. *Developmental Psychology, 29,* 10–36.

Heikamp, T., Trommsdorff, G., Druey, M., Hübner, R. & von Suchodoletz, A. (2013). Kindergarten children's attachment security, inhibitory control, and the internalization of rules of conduct. *Frontiers in Psychology, 4(133).*

Hirsh-Pasek, K., Golinkoff, R. M., Berk, L., & Singer, D.G. (2009). *A mandate for playful learning in preschool.* New York: Oxford University Press.

John-Steiner, V., & Mahn, H. (1996). Sociocultural approaches to learning and development: A Vygotskian framework. *Educational Psychologist, 31,* 191–206.

Klein, T. P., Wirth, D., & Linas, K. (2003). Play: Children's context for development. *Young Children, 58,* 38–45.

Kochanska, G., Philibert, R. A., & Barry, R. A. (2009). Interplay of genes and early mother-child relationship in the development of self-regulation from toddler to preschool age. *Journal of Child Psychology and Psychiatry, 50,* 1331–1338.

Kopp, C. B. (1982). Antecedents of self-regulation: A developmental perspective. *Developmental Psychology, 18,* 199–214.

Le Doux, J. (2002). *Synaptic self: How our brains become who we are.* New York: Viking.

Lieberman, A. (1993). *The emotional life of the toddler.* New York: Free Press.

Matricciani, L., Olds, T., & Petkov, J. (2012). In search of lost sleep: Secular trends in the sleep time of school-aged children and adolescents. *Sleep Medicine Reviews, 16,* 203–211.

Miller, E., & Almon, J. (2009). *Crisis in the kindergarten: Why children need to play in school.* College Park, MD: Alliance for Childhood.

Mindell, J. A., Sadeh, A., Kohyama, J., & How, T. H. (2010). Parental behaviors and sleep outcomes in infants and toddlers: A cross-cultural comparison. *Sleep Medicine, 11,* 393–399.

Mischel, W., Ozlem, A., Berman, M., Casey, B. J., Gotlib, I., Jonides, J., & Shoda, Y. (2011). "Willpower" over the life span: Decomposing self-regulation. *Social Cognitive and Affective Neuroscience, 6,* 252–256.

National Scientific Council on the Developing Child. (2004). *Young children develop in an environment of relationships.* Working Paper No. 1. Retrieved from http://www.developingchild.net.

Nelson, C. A., Furtado, E. A., Fox, N. A., & Zeanah, C. H. (2009). The deprived human brain. *American Scientist, 97,* 222–229.

Noble, K., Houston, S., Kan, E., & Sowell E. (2012). Neural correlates of socioeconomic status in the developing human brain. *Developmental Science, 15,* 516–527.

Ochsner, K. N., Silvers, J. A., & Buhle, J. T. (2012). Functional imaging studies of emotion regulation: A synthetic review and evolving model of the cognitive control of emotion. *Annals of the New York Academy of Sciences, 1251,* E1–E24.

Potegal, M., Kosorok, M., & Davidson, R. (2003). Temper tantrums in young children: 2. tantrum duration and temporal organization. *Developmental and Behavioral Pediatrics, 24,* 148–154.

Rothbart, M. K., Ahadi, S. A., & Hershey, K. L. (1994). Temperament and social behavior in childhood. *Merrill-Palmer Quarterly, 40,* 21–39.

Sadeh, A. (2001). *Sleeping like a baby: A sensitive and sensible approach to solving your child's sleep problems.* New Haven, CT: Yale University Press.

Salonen, P., Vauras, M., & Efklides, A. (2005). Social interaction—What can it tell us about metacognition and coregulation in learning? *European Psychologist, 10,* 199–208.

Schore, A. N. (2001). The effects of early relational trauma on right brain development, affect regulation, and infant mental health. *Infant Mental Health Journal, 22,* 201–269.

Shimm, P., & Ballen, K. (1995). *The toddler years: The experts' guide to the tough and tender years.* New York: Da Capo.

Shonkoff, J. P., & Garner, A. S. (2012). The lifelong effects of early childhood adversity and toxic stress. *Pediatrics, 129,* 232–246.

Shonkoff, J. P., & Phillips, D. A. (2000). *From neurons to neighborhoods: The science of early childhood development.* Washington, DC: National Academy Press.

Solomon C. R., & Serres, F. (1999). Effects of Parental Verbal Aggression on Children's Self-Esteem and School Marks. *Child Abuse & Neglect, 23,* 339–351.

Sroufe, A. (2005). Attachment and development: A prospective, longitudinal study from birth to adulthood. *Attachment & Human Development, 7,* 349–367.

Tegano, D. W., Sawyers, J. K., & Moran, J. D. (1989). Problem finding and solving in play: The role of the teacher. *Childhood Education, 66,* 92–97.

Vogler, P., Crivello, G., & Woodhead, M. (2008). Early childhood transitions research: A review of concepts, theory, and practice. Working Paper No. 48. The Hague: Bernard van Leer Foundation.

Vygotsky, L. S. (1978). *Mind in society: The development of higher psychological processes.* Cambridge, MA: Harvard University Press.

Waters, S. F., Virmani, E. A., Thompson, R. A., Meyer, S. M., Raikes, H. A., & Jochem, R. (2010). Emotion regulation and attachment: Unpacking two constructs and their association. *Journal of Psychopathology & Behavioral Assessment*, 32, 37–47.

Index

Index

Index

Index

Index

About the Author

Tovah P. Klein, PhD, is director of the Barnard College Center for Toddler Development and a psychology professor at Barnard College, Columbia University. For more than two decades she has worked with parents and toddlers. Her research explores parenting challenges; children's play; sleep and separation; and child trauma. She writes for and is frequently quoted in the media, including the *New York Times, Washington Post,* Parents.com, and Slate.com. She consults worldwide to programs for young children, has been a developmental advisor for *Sesame Street,* and is on the advisory boards of Room to Grow, Ubuntu Education Fund, Rwanda Educational Assistance Project, Learnnow.org, and PerDev. She lives in New York with her husband and three children.